A
SOUTHERN ELECTRIC
ALBUM

MICHAEL WELCH

Capital Transport

ISBN 1 85414 270 4

Published by Capital Transport Publishing, 38 Long Elmes, Harrow Weald, Middlesex

Printed by CS Graphics, Singapore

Introduction

My first experience of Southern Region third-rail operations was in the mid-1950s when my parents moved to Worthing and since that time I have always lived within earshot of an electric railway line. My primary interest in railways, I must confess, has always been the steam locomotive though I have always grudgingly accepted that, of all the principal forms of railway propulsion, electric traction was by far the most modern and efficient and, most importantly in this day and age, probably the least environmentally damaging. This tolerance of electric trains was explained by a friend many years ago. He possessed an extremely vivid imagination and stated that electric traction was really a sophisticated form of steam power, the only difference being that the 'steam power' (from a steam-driven electricity generating station) was provided by means of a cable!

By late 1958 I had become a regular West Coast Line patron, travelling to school in Brighton, usually in 2-BIL/2-HAL stock. The latter units were rather unappealing, with their uncomfortable bench-type seats and awful painted interiors, but at least both of these pre-war types were reliable, which is more than can be said for some 'modern' trains. The coastal lines radiating from Brighton often seemed to be saddled with stock approaching life expiry (and sometimes beyond it!) and the next type to appear on those routes was the 4-CORs, which replaced the 2-BIL/2-HAL units. They only lasted a short time before being ousted by Southern Railway-designed 2-HAPs in 1972. The latter units, and especially the driving trailers (DTCs), were leftovers from the Bulleid era and many of their design features, such as the internal compartment sliding doors and large single-paned windows, were reminiscent of his locomotive-hauled vehicles. These interesting units served the 'Coastway' routes from Brighton until BR Standard 2-HAPs took over in 1976, these in turn giving way to 4-CIG/4-VEP stock in 1982. Most trains to and from London had, of course, been formed of 4-CIG/4-BIG units since the mid-1960s, these units being supplemented by 4-CEP/4-BEP plus 4-COR/4-BUF formations on rush-hour services and I must have clocked up thousands of miles on these types commuting to and from Croydon. I have always been a great fan of the 4-CIG units which, in my view, offer a reasonably smooth ride (provided one avoided the motor coach!), plush and spacious seating and even the luxury of compartment accommodation for both first and second class passengers. Fortunately, when the 4-CIGs were refurbished in the 1980s many of the mistakes made with the 4-CEPs, such as the uncomfortable new seating and very draughty hopper windows, were wisely avoided. Sadly, in recent years many of the 4-CIG units employed on the Brighton Line have been affected by persistent vandalism, not to mention considerable damage inflicted by 'runaway' refreshment trolleys, and the passenger accommodation of many is in poor shape. Despite this, these units would still receive my vote as the best produced during the period covered by this album. Regrettably, in recent years, Mk1 'slam door' stock has been constantly attacked in the media but, in my experience, the old units are still extremely reliable in service, another factor in their favour that is never mentioned. I have been lucky enough to have participated on 'farewell' railtours commemorating the end of the 4-GRI and 4-COR units and travelled on the last 'ordinary' 4-EPB working on 31st March 1995, but it will be a particularly sad day when the 4-CIGs finally bow out.

Compiling this album has been a very enjoyable experience, this enjoyment being heightened by the kind assistance I have received from many people, especially the photographers who had the foresight to take pictures of electric trains at a time when steam was still all the rage. Some former colleagues in the SR CM&EE Dept. Maintenance Control (Maintrol) have been most helpful I would like to thank Chris Evans, Malcolm Pocknell, Steve Rogers and Glen Woods for allowing me to 'pick their brains' on occasions. In addition, John Atkinson, Terence Barry, Graham Burtenshaw and David Fakes have kindly read the proof, and suggested many corrections and improvements which have enhanced the end result. I accept responsibility for any errors that have remained undetected.

Michael Welch,
Burgess Hill, West Sussex.
February 2003

Contents

South Western Division

A 1937- or 1946-built unit? The 4-COR stock was basically a pre-war design, but during the Second World War naval installations at Portsmouth were repeatedly bombed by German planes and an unwelcome side-effect of this action was the extensive damage inflicted upon railway property. Portsmouth Harbour station was hit by German bombs in August 1940, badly damaging the new station, the rebuilding of which had only been finished three years previously. On the night of 10th/11th January 1941 the Luftwaffe struck again, almost completely destroying the station premises. Some of the tracks, which are built on piers above the harbour's choppy waters, were severed in the attack, leaving some coaches of 4-COR unit No.3132 stranded: the vehicles were abandoned until the war ended. Fratton depot also suffered direct hits, causing widespread damage to rolling stock. During the hostilities a total of 25 coaches from 4-COR stock, and associated units, was lost as a result of enemy action and these were replaced in 1946 by vehicles built to the original design. Some units were totally destroyed, including No.3119, seen here forming the leading unit of the 6.20pm Waterloo to Portsmouth Harbour train at Woking on 17th August 1966. So, appearances can be deceptive and this unit was actually of more recent construction than its appearance suggests! *Trevor Owen*

Waterloo to Weymouth

The overhead signal box and maze of tracks in the far distance (not to mention the station nameboard!) immediately identify this location as Clapham Junction, Great Britain's busiest railway station. The train consists of a 4-TC/3-TC/4-REP combination, with the last unit nearest to the camera, and this picture was taken on 24th December 1968. Unfortunately, this is something of a mystery working because, contrary to usual operating practice, the 4-REP is formed at the country end and the train is travelling on the up local line, the nearby up fast track being occupied by a train formed of (what appears to be) 4-COR stock. Maybe the TC/REP formation was empty stock, because the rear coach does not appear to be carrying any passengers. The signal box is Clapham Junction 'A' box, which partially collapsed on the morning of 10th May 1965, causing one of the most severe dislocations to services ever seen on the South Western Division (SWD). *Colour-Rail*

Electro-diesel locomotive No.E6108, seen here posing at Clapham Junction on 2nd October 1971, was originally built at Doncaster Works as orthodox electric locomotive No.E5005 for the Kent Coast electrification scheme. It entered traffic in May 1959, based at Stewarts Lane shed for use on both passenger and freight duties. When electrification of the Bournemouth Line was approved the Southern Region (SR) operating authorities identified a need for additional motive power mainly for boat train and miscellaneous freight workings, and it was decided to convert ten E5000 class (later Class 71) locomotives to electro-diesels by installing a 650hp diesel engine. The locomotives were modified at Crewe Works and No.E6108 entered service on 6th May 1968, one of its first duties reportedly being haulage of the 9.57 a.m. Waterloo to Weymouth Quay boat train as far as Bournemouth a few days later. Unfortunately, the converted locomotives were not very reliable and, in addition, boat train traffic had already started to decline as the shipping companies lost out to the airlines. It was decided that the few trains operated by these machines could be worked by other locomotives and the last of the Class 74s, as they had become, were condemned at the end of 1977. *Frank Hornby*

Electrification of the Bournemouth Line, approved by the government in September 1964, was the first major scheme for the development of rail traffic to be given the 'green light' during the Beeching regime. It was clear from the outset, however, that capital costs had been pared to the bare minimum, the decision not to electrify the Bournemouth to Weymouth stretch being an indication of this approach. The scheme entailed electrifying 80 route miles from Brookwood to Bournemouth Central, together with a further short section to provide access to a new maintenance depot at Branksome. Considerable investment in resignalling and new sub-stations was also involved. It was decided that push-pull operation would be employed. In the early 1960s the SR had conducted high-speed trials to ascertain the feasibility of push-pull working and had satisfied the government's inspecting officers that this arrangement, which was quite novel at the time, was feasible and, most of all, safe. The SR envisaged using a high-powered electric 'tractor' unit which would be marshalled at the London end of a Waterloo to Weymouth train, the remaining units being unpowered. On arrival at Bournemouth the leading non-powered unit would be detached and carry on to Weymouth behind a modified BRCW Type 3 diesel locomotive. On the return trip the unit would be propelled to Bournemouth and attached to the rear of a London-bound train while the diesel engine was uncoupled. The eleven high-powered 'tractor' units were known as 4-REPs (restaurant electro-pneumatic) and were formed driving motor second, trailer restaurant buffet, trailer brake first plus another driving motor second. The motor coaches were new build, whereas the trailer vehicles were converted, mostly at York carriage works, from existing locomotive-hauled Mk.1 stock. Each motor coach was equipped with four 400hp traction motors, thus giving a total power output of 3,200hp for each twelve-car formation. Most unusually, the guard's compartment was located in a trailer coach. Regular 4-REP/TC operation was introduced on 3rd April 1967 and for a brief period the Bournemouth Line could boast of five different types of motive power: steam, 4-REP/TC, EDL/TC, Type 3 diesel/TC and Brush Type 4. In this photograph 4-REP No.3009 is seen approaching Wimbledon with two trailer units in tow on 8th June 1967. Electrification of the Bournemouth route was a major commercial success for BR, and in 1974 the service was enhanced and a further four 4-REP and six 4-TC units were constructed, though it should be noted that three of the latter were 3-TC reforms. *R. C. Riley*

A major point of interest on the Bournemouth Line during the period covered by this book was the yard at Micheldever which was used by the SR to store damaged or withdrawn vehicles. The yard occupied the site of a former chalk quarry and its closeness to Eastleigh Works, plus its isolated location away from any centre of population, were distinct advantages. The incredible variety of rolling stock that could be seen at the yard is apparent in this shot taken on 31st July 1965. The most prominent vehicle is a 4-SUB motor coach, but a rake of former London Transport tube stock, presumably awaiting refurbishment for use on the Isle of Wight, is also visible plus a number of (what appear to be) horseboxes. The 4-SUB motor coach is No.S8144S which was originally part of a three-car '1285' Class unit built in 1925 for the Waterloo to Guildford via Cobham service. It was constructed by the Metropolitan Carriage Wagon & Finance Co. Ltd. and had seven third class compartments and weighed 39 tons. These units had the very distinctive 'wedge-end' as seen here and were originally numbered 1285 to 1310. In 1945/46 the units were augmented with newly-built ten compartment trailer thirds, which were largely of steel construction, and renumbered 4300 to 4325. The vehicle depicted was marshalled in unit No.4308 which was in the final batch withdrawn in January 1962 following replacement by BR Standard 4-EPB units. An identical vehicle is preserved as part of the National Collection at York. *David Wigley*

In complete contrast to the previous picture, showing a coach that was 40 years old, the unit depicted here was almost brand new – note the shiny yellow-painted axlebox covers – when photographed working an up Bournemouth to Waterloo stopping train at Micheldever on 10th July 1967. The unit is 4-VEP No.7715, one of twenty built for high-density semi-fast services on the SWD. The driving trailer coaches were constructed at York Works while the other vehicles were built at Derby. All the remaining units of this type were built entirely at York. The formation of this stock is driving trailer composite, motor second brake, trailer second plus another driving trailer, providing 48 first and 232 second class seats. The stock is gangwayed throughout and English Electric traction equipment is employed, each Mk.6 motor bogie being fitted with two 250hp motors. *Colour-Rail*

Above Electric locomotive No.20002, looking resplendent following an overhaul, is seen at Eastleigh shed on 9th May 1959. This 99-ton machine was built at Ashford Works in September 1945 during the Bullied era, and was originally numbered CC2. Each axle was driven by a 245hp motor, giving a total output of 1,470hp. The locomotive was fitted with an electrically-heated boiler to supply steam for carriage heating and was also equipped with a pantograph. There were three engines of this type, but the last one to be built was heavier and incorporated considerable design differences. This class was probably most associated with the Victoria to Newhaven Harbour boat trains, but could also be observed on heavy freight workings from New Cross Gate and Norwood yards on the Central Division. For a very brief period in the mid-1960s they worked the Derby Day Royal Train from Victoria to Tattenham Corner. No.20002 was withdrawn in December 1968 and scrapped in September 1969 at Cashmore's yard at Newport in South Wales. *Trevor Owen*

Left A scene near Wallers Ash tunnel, between Micheldever and Winchester, showing an eight-car formation of suburban units heading south in February 1967. The leading unit is 4-EPB No.5220, while the other units appear to be two 2-EPBs. Unfortunately the train is unidentified, but is most likely to be a crew training or test running special, some of which certainly used headcode 75. During this time an intensive programme of training was in progress to familiarise operating staff with electric trains, even the old EPB suburban stock which was overhauled at Eastleigh Works and would therefore be worked by train crews based at SWD steam sheds. The third rail between Pirbright Junction and Swaythling was energised in mid-December 1966 and trial running with EPB units began almost immediately. Regular public services between Basingstoke and Waterloo started on 2nd January 1967 using a combination of 2-HAP/2-EPB units, hardly the best stock to convince Basingstoke commuters of the benefits of electric train travel, but presumably nothing else was available! *Trevor Owen*

Another picture taken at Eastleigh on 9th May 1959, this time showing electric locomotive No.E5003 inside the works for modification. This machine was one of 24 identical Bo-Bos constructed at Doncaster Works in 1959/60 for the Kent Coast electrification and this particular engine was taken into capital stock at Stewarts Lane depot in March 1959. These locomotives (later Class 71) were just over 50 feet long, weighed 77 tons in working order and each axle was powered by a 638hp motor, thus giving a total of 2,552hp. Built for both freight and passenger use, the locomotives included in their regular duties haulage of the prestigious 'Golden Arrow' Pullman-car train from London Victoria to Dover, and also the 'Night Ferry'. The latter was a unique working on BR, conveying through sleeping cars to the continent and, at one time, it was reputed to be the heaviest passenger train on BR, frequently loading to over 800 tons, so these engines had a justifiable claim to fame! No.E5003 lasted only until February 1967 in the guise seen here, because it was rebuilt at Crewe Works into electro-diesel No.E6107 for use on the Bournemouth Line. It was withdrawn as No.74 007 in December 1977 and cut-up at Birds, Long Marston, scrapyard in August 1978. *Trevor Owen*

A scene at Brockenhurst during the summer of 1967 showing 4-VEP No.7709 waiting in the down loop platform before departure to Lymington Pier. The section from Swaythling to Lymington was reportedly energised on 18th January 1967 and on the same day a test train was run from Wimbledon formed of an electro-diesel locomotive and some EPB units. The 5¼ miles-long Lymington branch is noteworthy for a number of reasons and is, perhaps, most famous because it became the last steam-worked passenger branch in Great Britain. Diesel units took over from steam traction on 3rd April 1967, but they were only a stopgap measure until electrification. Way back in 1938 the enterprising Southern Railway introduced the first 'drive on, drive off' ferry service between Yarmouth and Lymington. The branch is still operational and, at the time of writing, has a generous half-hourly service. *Colour-Rail*

The Bournemouth Line timetable introduced on 10th July 1967 involved eight traffic diagrams for 4-REP units, leaving only three units available for maintenance purposes. If a 4-REP was unavailable for a particular train it was, of course, possible to substitute an electro-diesel locomotive or BRCW Type 3 diesel, but it would not be possible to provide a buffet service. In the early days of the Bournemouth Line electric service the SR was clearly struggling to run the advertised timetable and this situation was exacerbated when the 4-REPs, which were booked to run around 12,000 miles per month, fell due for bogie overhauls at Chart Leacon depot, Ashford, leaving even fewer units to carry the passengers! In early 1968 it was decided that more resources were needed to relieve the pressure on the 4-REPs, and an eight-car unit was created solely for use on Waterloo to Bournemouth semi-fast services. It was composed of coaches from 4-VEP unit Nos.7739, 7741 and 7742 and made up of four driving trailer vehicles, three motor coaches and a loco-hauled restaurant buffet (RB) coach which was specially converted for emu operation. The unit, known as 8-VAB and numbered 8001, had 96 first and 299 second class seats plus 23 in the buffet car. The motor coach adjacent to the RB was tabled for the service of meals, so reducing its normal seating capacity. When four new 4-REP units were built for the augmented Bournemouth Line service which started in 1974, the 8-VAB became largely redundant and was often held 'spare' at Bournemouth depot, where it is seen on 10th January 1975, and was later disbanded. *Chris Evans*

Unlike the Waterloo to Bournemouth line, which has only moderate gradients, the section between Bournemouth and Weymouth has some of the stiffest inclines on the former SR, the 1 in 50 climb out of Weymouth being particularly difficult as it is not possible for trains to take a 'run' at the bank. Another considerable obstacle is Parkestone bank, between Poole and Bournemouth, with its sections of 1 in 60 against eastbound trains. In steam days a banker was sometimes provided for heavy trains. Here, BRCW Type 3 Bo-Bo No.D6520 is depicted propelling 4-TC unit No.417 up the bank towards Bournemouth on 1st April 1967. At that time the full Bournemouth Line service had not started, but 4-TCs were in widespread use throughout the SWD on a variety of services because the operating authorities were keen to reduce steam working to a minimum. Unit No.417 ran for some time with driving trailer second No.S76331 which had been experimentally refurbished with improved seating and fluorescent lighting. *Colour-Rail*

At first sight it may seem inappropriate to include 4-TC units in a book about SR electric stock but, in fact, these units were regarded by the SR as part of the emu fleet and were maintained as such. In this shot 4-TC unit No.418, hauled by 'standard' BRCW Type 3 No.D6551, is depicted approaching Radipole Halt on 1st July 1968 forming a down working. The headcode indicates a semi-fast train from Waterloo. The precise identity of this working is not known, nor the reason for the most unusual appearance of No.D6551, but it is possible that the Type 3 was a last-minute substitute for a push-pull fitted machine. Because of the long distances worked by these 4-TC units – Waterloo to Weymouth is 142 miles – and the fact that a very high proportion of the units was required for traffic purposes each day, for a long time this fleet was clocking up a remarkable average of 12,500 miles per unit every month, slightly higher than the 4-REPs. *Colin Caddy*

The new and the old order at Weymouth! An afternoon service to Waterloo, formed of 4-TC unit No.419, leaves Weymouth propelled by BRCW Type 3 No.D6536 on 6th July 1967 as a 'Merchant Navy' Class Pacific waits on the other line to take over the up Channel Islands boat train. This scene was recorded during the final week of steam operation on the 'Southern'. Note the very extensive layout at the approaches to Weymouth station, which has since been almost completely obliterated, with supermarkets and car parks now occupying much former railway land. The drab and uninspiring all-over blue livery applied to the new Bournemouth stock was much criticised and it was extremely difficult to keep it looking clean, let alone smart. The appearance of the units was undoubtedly improved when they were repainted in blue/grey colours. *R. C. Riley*

It is, perhaps, hard to believe that this is how Weymouth station looked in the late-1960s. Gas lighting, dilapidated wooden platform awnings and, apparently, a considerable amount of surplus land judging by the five tracks between the platforms. The premises were later rebuilt in modern style with more modest facilities. In this view, taken in the summer of 1969, 4-TC No.421 waits at Platform 3 prior to departure with a train to London, while the train on the right appears to be a Western Region dmu, probably forming a working to Westbury or Bristol via Yeovil. The 4-TCs were all converted from loco-hauled stock which was totally refurbished internally with new, re-profiled seats, formica panelling and luggage racks. Replacement metal reading lights were fitted, but incandescent lighting was retained. All of the units were equipped with B5(S) bogies to improve the riding. By the early 1970s air-conditioned rolling stock was becoming common on BR and the 4-TCs already compared unfavourably to stock used on similar medium distance journeys on the network, but were destined to last until the late 1980s, by which time some of the vehicles were nearing their fortieth birthday! *Colour-Rail*

Waterloo to Portsmouth

The 4-COR units were universally known as 'Nelsons' due to their long association with the Waterloo to Portsmouth line plus their single windscreen which gave them a 'one-eye' look, and in this view unit No.3160 is seen rushing through Esher at the head of an up twelve-car train in the mid-1960s. The headcode indicates a special from Portsmouth & Southsea to Waterloo. At the time of this picture No.3160 was a newly-formed unit, being made up of surplus motor coaches from disbanded 4-RES units plus assorted trailer carriages from withdrawn Brighton Line six-car units. This supposedly 'new' unit must have caused considerable consternation to train watchers of the day thumbing through their spotters' books. In reality, it was rather old and destined for early withdrawal once replacement stock was available. *Geoff Rixon*

Another view taken at Woking on 17th August 1966. The unit seen here is 2-HAP No.6140, one of a batch (Nos.6106 to 6146) built in 1961 for Phase Two of the Kent Coast electrification scheme. At this time the SR tended to use most units indiscriminately throughout the system, hence the appearance of this unit at the front of the 6.05pm from Waterloo to Portsmouth commuter working, somewhat removed from the services for which it was intended! Ironically some of these units, Nos.6147 to 6173, were constructed for use on the South Western Division but, presumably, at the time of this picture most were actually operating on the South Eastern! The inverted triangle, indicating the position of the unit's brake van, was an aid to platform staff. *Trevor Owen*

The 2-BIL units were a familiar sight on the Portsmouth Direct Line for more than 30 years, and in this photograph an extremely smart looking No.2017 is seen forming the front unit of a Waterloo to Portsmouth & Southsea stopping train near Witley in June 1967. Note the heavily wooded countryside being traversed by the train, this being typical of the Waterloo to Portsmouth line, south of Guildford. The tight curve is a less welcome feature of this notoriously sinuous route, which is infested with some quite severe permanent speed restrictions. Appropriately, unit No.2017 was built for use on this line, unit Nos.2011 to 2048 being constructed in 1936 for the Waterloo to Alton/Portsmouth electrification scheme. Initially they were numbered 1901–20/1954–71 but these numbers were altered before they entered traffic. No.2017 was one of a large batch of these units withdrawn in 1970 as the 4-VEPs entered service, but at least it had a very good innings! *Trevor Owen*

This picture, taken near Witley on 16th October 1966, shows 4-GRI No.3086 forming the rear unit of an unidentified Portsmouth Harbour to Waterloo train. The front set appears to be a 4-COR in blue livery. Unit No.3086 began life as a 4-RES, being built in early 1937 for the Portsmouth Line electrification scheme. The original formation consisted of a motor coach, trailer first corridor, kitchen/dining car and another motor coach. The motor coaches were constructed by the Southern Railway, but the trailer first vehicles were built by Metropolitan Cammell whilst the kitchen coaches were built by the Birmingham Railway Carriage & Wagon Co. There were 104 third class seats, 30 first and a total of 48 seats was provided for dining purposes. The dining accommodation consisted of 36 seats in the kitchen/dining coach and 12 in a small saloon at the end of the trailer first carriage that was formed adjacent to the kitchen car. The main part of the trailer first coach consisted of five compartments with a lavatory at each end of the compartment section. The unit ran in this guise as No.3065 until early 1961 when it was decided to convert the kitchen vehicle into a griddle car for serving hot snacks, which was the latest bright idea in railway catering at the time. It returned to traffic in 1962 and a total of three units was converted, modification of the remainder of the fleet apparently being ruled out on financial grounds. In December 1963 the units were renumbered in a separate series and No.3065 became No.3086, surviving until the early 1970s when 4-CIG/4-BIG stock replaced them. *Trevor Owen*

Photographed on a beautiful spring day with the lineside trees just coming into leaf, 4-COR unit No.3120 threads Liss forest at the head of a 12-car Portsmouth Harbour to Waterloo fast train on 30th April 1966. Full electric passenger services commenced on this route on 4th July 1937, but the first electric passenger-carrying workings took place prior to this date. Trial running to Fratton depot reportedly started on 8th March, but the first public working took place on 19th May when electric stock formed two return services from Waterloo to Portsmouth which were run as reliefs to scheduled steam services. 4-COR stock was also used for excursions from May, but the new stock did not start regular operation of selected trains (to steam timings) until 5th June 1937. By the time the full electric service was introduced most operating staff were probably used to the new trains and the first day of the electric timetable is reported to have gone without a hitch. *Neville Simms*

Below right A passengers' eye view of part of Portsmouth & Southsea station's low level platforms taken in early 1970, depicting electric stock that was soon to disappear from the scene. From left to right the units shown are 2-BIL No.2029, 2-HAL No.2619 and 4-COR No.3106. The most interesting unit in the shot is undoubtedly the 2-BIL and it is unfortunate that so little can be seen of its driving trailer coach, No.S12109S. This was originally formed in unit No.2008 and was transferred to No.2029 when the two units permanently exchanged driving trailers in 1951. The first ten 2-BIL units differed in some respects to the other batches, in addition to being slightly longer they were originally equipped with Metropolitan Vickers traction motors, but these were replaced with English Electric motors in the 1950s. The coach interiors had bright cream-painted corridor panels, unlike the later series which had varnished wood. Note the door ventilation louvre above the window, another design difference which gave Nos.2001–2010 a very distinctive external appearance. The latter units were earmarked for early withdrawal when the 2-BILs started to be scrapped and it seems that this vehicle was among the last of the original coaches in service. *Gerald Daniels*

Above A stopping train from Waterloo to Portsmouth sprints along west of Bedhampton Halt on 2nd March 1963. The front unit is No.2134, which was one of the final series (unit Nos.2117 to 2152) built between August and November 1938 for the Waterloo to Reading/Guildford via Ascot electrification scheme. It appears that No.2134 led a completely uneventful career, not blemished by its involvement in a mishap of any kind. It was withdrawn in 1970, yet another victim of the mass introduction of the 4-VEP stock. *Trevor Owen*

Engineering work on Sundays has been a feature of the railway scene for a long time, not to mention the cause of many complaints, and in this view the diverted 8.50am Waterloo to Portsmouth Harbour train is depicted passing Chertsey on a rather gloomy 30th October 1966. The leading unit is 4-COR No.3132 which was the unfortunate unit marooned at Portsmouth Harbour from January 1941 until the end of the war. This was a result of enemy bombing which severed the tracks. The train had presumably been re-routed via Staines due to track work on the main line and passengers destined for the Isle of Wight were doubtless already wondering whether they would miss their ferry connection. Note the fine Italianate station building which was reputedly modelled on Netley, in Hampshire. In the early years Chertsey was the terminus of a branch line from Weybridge, but when the line was extended to Virginia Water in 1864 the new station was built on a different site. Amazingly, there was a small locomotive shed here until 1937. *Trevor Owen*

Waterloo to Alton

A Waterloo to Alton train, led by 2-HAL unit No.2608, approaches Esher in February 1967. Two units of this type were withdrawn many years before programmed withdrawals commenced; No.2646 was disbanded in 1948, while No.2680 was a victim of an accident at Chatham in April 1956. Unit No.2608 was unlucky enough to become the third unit to be withdrawn, following a collision at Lovers Walk depot, Brighton, in June 1967. It was clearly only slightly damaged, however, its trailer replacing 2-BIL unit No.2123's trailer vehicle while its motor coach was subsequently converted to de-icing vehicle No.DS70268. No.2608 was one of 76 units built in 1938/39 for the Gillingham and Maidstone electrification schemes. These units were built using hardwood body frames with steel panelling and wood and canvas roofs, which featured domed driving ends. The motor coaches had seven third class non-corridor compartments, each seating ten passengers, while the driving trailer vehicles had a side corridor giving access to four first class, four third class compartments and a lavatory. The interiors and seating were rather spartan, especially in the third class where the comfortable cushions of previous designs had been replaced with hard, narrow bench-type seating, which was presumably considered adequate for Eastern Section customers. The comfort of the first class accommodation was reasonable, but not up to previous standards. The 2-HAL fleet was replaced by 4-VEP units between 1969 and 1971. *Geoff Rixon*

A picture taken at the west end of Woking station on 17th August 1966, showing the 5.39pm Waterloo to Alton train leaving, formed of a splendid assortment of stock. The twelve car formation comprises of a 2-EPB, unit No.5669, three BR-designed 2-HAP units and a unit on the rear which appears to be a 4-EPB. The 2-EPB was one of a series of 34 sets (Nos. 5651 to 5684) built on underframes from withdrawn 2-NOL units, these being the last SR units to be constructed in this way. They were, however, the first units to be built entirely without compartment accommodation, a radical departure from previous designs. This stock was built for the SWD and was especially associated with the Windsor Line services. The motor coach consisted of two four-bay saloons, one of which was non-smoking, while the driving trailer provided one four-bay and one five-bay saloon giving a total seating capacity of 178. The first units were noted under construction at Eastleigh Carriage Works in August 1959 and Nos. 5651 to 5659 entered service on 2nd October 1959: all of the remainder had been commissioned by March 1960. In the early 1980s many units were given a 'facelift' (refurbishment of the passenger accommodation) which included the installation of fluorescent lighting. *Trevor Owen*

4-SUB No.4111, seen here leading an Alton train away from Woking also on 17th August 1966, was the first all-steel unit of its type (the first ten had wood and canvas roofs) and was outshopped from Eastleigh Works in April 1946. It was the first to be built of a second batch of ten units, these being all-compartment stock with a total seating capacity of 420, considerably fewer than the prototype units which managed to cram 468 passengers aboard in what must have been extremely uncomfortable conditions. One compartment trailer in each unit was built with six wide compartments which could be converted to first class if required. The same curved, wide bodyside profile was used, but unlike the earlier units the second batch had almost flat front ends, the domed cab roof design being abandoned. The front panels continued right up to roof level, a design feature that became standard practice for some years. While the all-steel construction was revolutionary on the 'Southern', the compartment accommodation necessitated the use of hinged 'slam' doors in contrast to London Transport's progressive policy of saloons with air-operated sliding doors, and it had been said that in some respects the units were outdated before they left the drawing board. Naturally, the older 4-SUB stock was the first to be withdrawn and No.4111 lasted until May 1972. *Trevor Owen*

Waterloo to Reading

A scene at Queens Road, Battersea, station (which is out of sight behind the train) showing a rake of 2-BIL/2-HAL units heading towards Clapham Junction with a Waterloo to Reading/Aldershot working. This shot was taken on 26th July 1959. The bridge in the background carries the Brighton Line tracks into Victoria. The substantial layout seen here consists of four pairs of tracks: the slow and fast lines to and from Wimbledon are in the foreground, while the tracks furthest from the camera are the fast Windsor lines with the slow Windsor lines on the extreme left. The train in view is travelling along the down fast Windsor line. *R. C. Riley*

A four-coach Reading to Waterloo train approaches Barnes on 25th March 1962, with 2-HAL unit No.2659 leading. The tracks on the right are those to Brentford and Hounslow (commonly known as the 'Hounslow Loop') which eventually rejoin the 'main' Reading line at Feltham, where there was a triangular junction giving access towards Reading and Twickenham. When the Southern Railway was deciding its electric unit codes it seemed to have an obsession with toilet facilities. There were bi-lavatory units (2-BILs), half-lavatory units (2-HALs) and, curiously, even those with no lavatory (2-NOLs) were incorporated into the system. Unfortunately, the 4-LAVs broke all of the rules, the code misleadingly suggesting that all of the coaches had a lavatory whereas, in reality, there were only two toilets per unit, located at opposite ends of the same vehicle! *R. C. Riley*

In this portrait, recorded just west of Twickenham station on 5th September 1970, a six-car formation of 2-BIL/2-HAL units heads westwards on a Waterloo to Reading train. The leading unit is 2-HAL No.2675 which was withdrawn from service before the end of the year, so it did not last long after this photograph was taken. It was built during the first half of 1939 for the Maidstone/Gillingham electrification scheme. The bridge carries the up Kingston loop line across the tracks; the down line is just visible between the bridge supports. This unit is depicted elsewhere in this album working on the South Eastern Section in 1959. *David Wigley*

Ascot to Guildford

This charming everyday scene at Frimley station, recorded on 22th September 1962, shows passengers waiting on the platform as 2-BIL unit No.2145 enters at the head of a train to Aldershot. Judging by the number of people on the other platform, and the signal in the 'off' position, a train was also due towards Ascot. Note the gas lighting and seaside holiday posters. No.2145 was one of the last batch of these units (Nos. 2117 to 2152), constructed at Eastleigh between August and November 1938 for the Waterloo to Reading/Ascot to Guildford electrification so, by coincidence, it is seen working on the line for which it was built! No.2145 had an unlucky war, being damaged at Fratton in May 1941 and again at Brighton in May 1943. At the time of this picture it had a further eight years of service remaining, being one of a large number of these units withdrawn in 1970. *Alan Jarvis*

The SR electric system was not famous for single lines, perhaps the best known being sections of the West Croydon to Wimbledon line and the Haywards Heath to Horsted Keynes branch, which was partially worked as a single line towards the end of its life. The Ascot to Ash Vale line also incorporates one of the few electrified single line sections, so a brief description of the history of this rather obscure route might be appropriate. The route was proposed by the LSWR as a means of connecting Windsor with Aldershot, and received parliamentary approval in 1873. It opened throughout on 2nd June 1879 as a single line route, but was later doubled between Ascot and Frimley Junction, where spurs were laid linking with the Bournemouth Line. The stretch south of Frimley was not converted and remains single track. In this interesting picture the driver of 2-BIL unit No.2038 has just surrendered the token for the single line section at Frimley Junction on 5th September 1970. Today there are probably more electrified single line stretches than ever, with the Lymington and Seaford branches springing immediately to mind, plus parts of the Weymouth route beyond Poole, in addition to the line depicted here. *David Wigley*

A four-car Aldershot to Guildford train leaves Ash station, which is just discernible in the distance, on 15th June 1963. The front unit is 2-BIL No.2091, while an unidentified 2-HAL brings up the rear. This route is, perhaps, better known as the Reading to Redhill line, a largely unelectrified cross-country route, apart from a few short sections. One of these is the stretch between Ash and Guildford, which was electrified (as previously mentioned in this album) as part of the 1938 Waterloo to Reading scheme. Today this line is served by Ascot to Guildford via Aldershot trains, with a token rush-hour through service to Waterloo over parts of the route. Unit No.2091 was built in 1937 for the Mid-Sussex line electrification and remained in traffic until 1969. *Trevor Owen*

Right This attractive period study of 4-SUB No.4506 threading Clapham cutting on 24th May 1958 recalls the early days of Southern Railway electrification. The unit comprises of really vintage coaches originally built for LBSCR overhead a.c. electric services between 1912 and 1924. In the late 1920s the a.c. stock was mostly converted to three-car units for d.c. third rail operation on suburban services and numbered in the series 1702 to 1772. When the latter were withdrawn in the mid-1950s those vehicles that were in relatively sound structural condition were reformed into eighteen four-car sets numbered 4501 to 4518. The coaches depicted were previously formed in three-car unit Nos.1728/31/34. Shortly after unit No.4506 was put together one of its motor coaches was withdrawn and replaced by another vehicle, this probably accounting for the 'odd' motor coach, without bonnets on the doors, at the rear of the train. It was anticipated that these units would only be required in traffic for a year or two before more modern stock replaced them, and the unit's smart external appearance is probably deceptive, more likely the result of a 'revarnish' rather than a full repaint which would normally be undertaken only as part of a heavy repair. By late 1959 many of the remaining units, often referred to as the 'Brighton' 4-SUBs on account of their ancestry, were reported to be in poor condition and out of regular use. No.4506 was withdrawn in December 1959, while the last units in service were condemned during the following month. *R. C. Riley*

A very rare and most interesting picture, showing 4-SUB No.4352 approaching Clapham Junction with (what appears to be) a train from Waterloo to Effingham Junction on 2nd July 1960. This was one of a series of 55 units (Nos. 4300 to 4354) formed just after the Second World War from 1925-built Maunsell three-car electric stock. Nos. 4300 to 4325 were formed from wedge-ended Western Section units, but the last batch was made up of flat-ended former Eastern Section stock, formerly Nos. 1496 to 1524, of the type seen here. The motor coaches were built by the Metropolitan Carriage Wagon & Finance Co. Ltd, while the trailer vehicles were constructed by the BRCW Co. They had steel panelled bodies on teak framing and the motor coaches contained eight third class compartments. The trailer carriages originally had seven first and two third class compartments, giving a total of 56 first and 180 third class seats. The traction motors were supplied by English Electric and other electrical equipment was provided by Metropolitan Vickers. A particularly interesting design feature was the compartment lights which were enclosed in glass bowls. In the mid-1940s all of the units were augmented with ten-compartment steel-bodied trailer third coaches, and renumbered as previously mentioned. This increased the total number of seats to 370 (with minor variations). The 'new' units were 257ft 5ins long. A total of 21 units remained operational in October 1960, and ten were still active a year later, but were quickly eliminated by the introduction of further BR Standard 4-EPB stock. *Frank Hornby*

South Western Suburban

A fascinating shot of 4-SUB No.4501 leaving Queens Road, Battersea, on 26th July 1959, the old letter headcode indicating a service around the Kingston loop via Teddington. No.4501 was a real delight to any coaching stock aficionado, and probably had the most colourful history of any unit featured in this album. The 'original' No.4501 was formed in May 1947 from 3-car unit 1534 and steel-bodied trailer No.S10341S, but this lasted only until March 1951 when the latter coach was transferred to No.4722 and the unit was disbanded. The second No.4501 was created in June 1956 using coaches from three withdrawn units, two converted former LBSCR a.c. electric coaches from unit Nos. 4254 and 4526 plus two *ex*-LSWR vehicles from unit No.4573. The latter (Nos. S9656S and S9815S) were almost unique in having *ex*-LSWR steam bodies, lengthened by the Southern Railway, and mounted on a.c. electric underframes. The second No.4501 became the very last surviving electric unit with pre-grouping bodywork to run in service and was withdrawn at Christmas 1959. It was cut-up with almost indecent haste at Newhaven during the following month, a sad end to an extremely interesting unit. *R. C. Riley*

Despite the profusion of 4-SUB units on the South Western and Central divisions throughout the period covered by this book (not to mention a few on the South Eastern), very few pictures of these workhorses were, alas, submitted for inclusion in this album. Perhaps the units had become such a familiar part of the everyday scene that most enthusiasts thought they would last for ever and failed to photograph them. With the benefit of hindsight, perhaps that was rather a pity. Full yellow ends became the rule in 1966, and it is thought that units repaired at Eastleigh were repainted blue from July 1966 so this picture of unit No.4298, in blue livery with a small yellow warning panel, is therefore of exceptional interest. It is recorded that only a small number of 4-SUB units were ever outshopped in this condition, so this picture is probably quite a rarity. No.4298 was photographed forming a Waterloo to Shepperton train in February 1967. *Trevor Owen*

When the LSWR opened its Nine Elms terminus it immediately found that an extension to the City of London was desirable. The section to Waterloo was opened in July 1848, but financial difficulties prevented any further progress, much to the frustration of passengers. This situation prompted the formation of an independent company, supported by the LSWR, who promoted a tube railway from Waterloo to the Bank, which was incorporated as the Waterloo & City Railway in 1893. Construction began in the following year and the 1 mile 46 chains-long line eventually opened on 8th August 1898 using rolling stock built in America and assembled at Eastleigh Works. In 1938 it was decided to modernise the line and new cars were constructed by English Electric. The twelve motor (40 seats) and sixteen trailer (52 seats) coaches were 47ft long with air-operated sliding doors and normally formed into five-car trains consisting of three trailer carriages with a motor coach at each end. In this rare glimpse of 'The Drain', as the line is colloquially known, car No.52 is seen waiting at Bank station on 25th April 1959. This car was a motor coach powered by two 190hp traction motors. *John Dewing*

The Waterloo & City Line

The Waterloo & City cars received running repairs at the small depot situated in the bowels of Waterloo station, where coaches could be lifted and defective bogies, motors and wheels changed as required. But heavy overhauls were only undertaken at main works and these were carried out at Lancing until the closure of the shops there in 1965, whereupon they were transferred to Eastleigh. The cars were brought to the surface using the W&C line's famous Armstrong hydraulic lift which was hidden away at the back of the main line station's Windsor Line platforms. Here, on a damp and dismal Saturday 20th March 1965, a coach is seen being raised to the surface before setting off on the long journey to Eastleigh. The photographer was a professional railwayman at the time and this intriguing shot was probably taken during an official visit to the W&C premises by the SR Lecture & Debating Society, membership of which was only available to BR staff. This part of the station has since been dramatically changed following the construction of the Eurostar terminus. *John Hayward*

Central Division

Without a doubt one of the most graceful railway structures in the south of England is the splendid Ouse Valley viaduct between Haywards Heath and Balcombe. This masterpiece of Victorian civil engineering, which was built in 1840/41, is 1,475 feet long, consists of 37 arches and eleven million bricks were reputedly used in its construction. Note the twin 'temples' or 'pavilions' (just visible on the right) at each end of the viaduct, which are well-known landmarks to travellers on the Brighton Line. The viaduct reportedly cost a trifling £38,500 to build! In this illustration, taken on 30th April 1972, the 6.45pm Brighton to Victoria fast train is seen heading across the viaduct in perfect evening sunshine. The train is comprised of a 4-BIG/4-CIG formation, the second vehicle being the 4-BIG's buffet car. Unfortunately, despite their popularity with passengers, the buffet cars were deemed to be uneconomic and are no longer seen on the Brighton Line. *John Scrace*

The Brighton Line

Looking at this picture it is sad to reflect that Victoria station's 'Brighton side' platforms were once bright and airy, despite the presence of polluting steam trains. Sadly, some years ago a massive shopping complex was built above this area and trains now leave from uninviting 'underground' platforms which have the atmosphere of a huge operating theatre, hardly a pleasant start to a railway journey! This picture was taken in more civilised times, on 24th April 1960, and shows 4-LAV unit No.2921 waiting on one of the 'middle roads', which greatly added to the station's operational flexibility by allowing trains to leave the inner ends of platforms while the outer ends were occupied. Unit No.2921 (originally numbered 1921) was the oldest of a distinctive fleet of 33 units that was built in 1931/32 for Brighton Line electrification scheme semi-fast and stopping services. It entered traffic in July 1932 when the first stage was completed to Reigate and Three Bridges. The units were generally formed of a seven compartment non-corridor motor coach with 70 seats, a side corridor composite trailer vehicle offering 30 first and 24 third class seats, a non-corridor trailer coach with 16 first and 70 third class seats and a further motor coach with seven compartments. This gave a total of 46 first and 234 third class seats, but it should be noted that the 4-LAV classification was misleading, because only two lavatories were provided and these were at opposite ends of the side corridor composite vehicle, which originally had a partition between the first and third class sections! The appearance of this stock was typical of Maunsell's style of that time, the curved bodysides with straight-sided guards' vans and motormen's cabs being unmistakable design features. Unlike his steam-hauled stock, however, the 4-LAVs were not fitted with guards' lookout duckets, but had periscopes instead. Remarkably, the units remained virtually unaltered throughout their lives. No.2921 was withdrawn in 1968, together with most of the other units, as new 4-VEP stock became available, but six units lingered until February 1969. After the removal of reusable components the units were sold to scrap dealers as far flung as Chesterfield, Newport (South Wales) and Wymondham, near Norwich. It should be noted that two more 4-LAV units were built in 1940, but they were modelled on the 2-HAL stock.
John Langford

A bird's-eye view of Victoria taken on 26th May 1970, but note the many changes that have occurred here during the ensuing years. The British Overseas Airways Corporation is defunct, Victoria station's signal box no longer functions while the train shed over the Brighton Line platforms was torn down (as previously mentioned) some years ago, and the Post Office tower is now closed to the public. Almost certainly, however, the unidentified 4-VEP seen pulling out of the station is still in service at the time of writing, well over 30 years after its introduction. It is likely that the unit was one of a series of 35 units (Nos. 7721 to 7755) constructed at York to replace the ageing 4-LAV stock on the Brighton Line and brought into service during 1968/69. The units consist of a driving trailer composite, trailer open second, motor second brake and another driving trailer. Unlike the 4-BIG/4-CIG stock, which preceded them, the first class sections were at the inner ends of the driving trailer vehicles. Originally, the units provided 48 first and 232 second class seats. In later years, however, one first class compartment in each driving trailer was converted to second and a small second class saloon replaced part of the large guard's compartment, so the number of second class seats has been considerably increased while the first class accommodation has been reduced. The somewhat spartan second class five-a-side seating and doors to each seating bay, which made the units extremely draughty, ensured that these units did not endear themselves to passengers, but at least they can carry enormous numbers of people, just the job at the height of the rush-hour.
John Scrace

In this shot 6-PUL unit No.3010 is seen passing Battersea Park with the mid-day Victoria to Brighton non-stop train on 2nd June 1965. This was one of 20 units constructed in 1932 for the London to Brighton/Worthing electrification and they included two saloon motor brake thirds, a trailer compartment third, two trailer compartment composites and a Pullman kitchen composite. Overall dimensions were 399ft long by 9ft 5in wide and each unit offered 72 first and 236 third class seats. The electrical equipment was by Metropolitan Vickers while the motors, somewhat unusually for the 'Southern', were 225hp 163-type provided by British Thomson-Houston. There were eight traction motors, four per motor coach, giving each unit a total of 1,800hp, so the units were extremely powerful. The motor coaches and Pullman cars were all-steel, the construction work being shared between the Metropolitan Carriage Wagon & Finance Co. Ltd. and the BRCW Co. The trailer vehicles were built at Eastleigh in the orthodox manner, however, consisting of teak body framing clad in galvanised steel sheeting, the roofs being canvas covered. Unlike earlier suburban stock, the intermediate coaches of which had a single buffer pressing against a rubbing block, these units were fitted with heavy self-contained side buffers throughout. This stock was phased out in the mid-1960s when replaced by 4-CIG/4-BIG units, but some individual vehicles survived a few years longer in the 6-COR units. *John Hayward*

Oh dear, what have they done to the 'Brighton Belle'? In the mid-1960s BR decided it was time for a 'new image' and embarked on a mission to give the organisation a nationwide corporate identity. Regrettably, this involved abandoning various regional colour schemes for rolling stock and repainting locomotives and coaches in decidedly drab and uninspiring blue or blue/grey livery. On the SR this involved painting main line units in blue and grey colours, which replaced the traditional green, a very durable and pleasant livery that had stood the all-important test of time very well. Unfortunately, it was also decreed that the 'Brighton Belle' Pullman vehicles would be repainted in the new 'corporate' blue and grey and, sadly, the attractive and distinctive umber and cream livery which had given these units such individuality, not to mention a high public profile, for a generation, gave way to the ghastly new colours. It was almost as if somebody in the BRB hierarchy was deliberately trying to make the 35 years-old units look ridiculous. Surely, if BR really wanted to change its image all it had to do was to run the trains on time! Here, 5-BEL unit No.3053 leads the ten-coach 3pm *ex*-Victoria past Thornton Heath on 8th August 1969, a mobile advertisement for a totally misguided and unpopular policy. *John Scrace*

The packed 5.23pm Victoria to Brighton commuter working, with 6-PAN unit No.3037 leading, threads Windmill Bridge Junction on a June evening in 1961. This stock was built in 1935 for the Eastbourne/Ore electrification and the general appearance of these units was similar to the earlier 6-PULs, the units being in the 3021 to 3037 number series. The formation was saloon motor brake third, corridor third, corridor first, pantry car, corridor third and another motor coach. This gave 72 first and 240 third class seats, the pantry car having 30 first class seats in five compartments. The all-steel motor coaches were built by contractors, but the other carriages were constructed by Eastleigh Carriage Works on frames built at Lancing, which was standard 'Southern' practice at the time. One noticeable difference between the 6-PUL and 6-PAN stock concerned the windows in the motor coaches. The former had ventilation louvres and droplights, while the latter were fitted with 'Airstream' sliding lights above the main windows, a novelty at the time, which supposedly drew fresh air into the coach while stale air was drawn out. Over the years some units exchanged vehicles as a result of mishaps. One unit, No.3032, was involved in a serious collision at Eastbourne in August 1958 and was subsequently disbanded. Some of the vehicles originally formed in this unit were later allocated to No.3014. *Paul Leavens*

Railway staff at East Croydon were probably resigned to the mundane and dreary business of serving thousands of ungrateful commuters, so the passage of the Derby Day 'Royal' from Victoria to Tattenham Corner always provided a welcome change from the usual routine. What a shame it was only an annual event! Photographed against the distant, but nonetheless distinctive, landmark of the Crystal Palace television aerial, electric locomotive No.20001 is seen passing Windmill Bridge Junction at the approach to East Croydon station on 31st May 1968. Naturally the rolling stock employed was in a different class to that used by ordinary mortals, and on this occasion consisted of (from the front) a Metro-Cammell Pullman car, the Royal saloon, another Pullman car and a BR Standard Mk.1 brake second coach. This picture gives an excellent view of the locomotive's rarely-used pantograph. The train is running along what was then the down fast line, with the former reversible line in the foreground. The position and status of these tracks was changed when the East Croydon layout was remodelled in the early 1980s: the fast lines would now be on the left of the shot. A lot of meticulous planning went into the running of this train and a special effort was made to ensure the 'Royal' had a clear 'road'. A stand-by locomotive was usually provided at Purley, just in case of an embarrassing failure. This was the last of four consecutive years that the Derby Day 'Royal' was worked by a Bulleid electric locomotive. *Chris Gammell*

Thirteen 4-BUF units were built at Eastleigh early in 1938 for the Mid-Sussex Line services, these units consisting basically of a 4-COR unit with the trailer third corridor coach replaced by a buffet car. The units were numbered 3072 to 3085, but it should be noted that No.3072 was a non-standard unit, seating 36 people in its buffet car and having a trailer first corridor coach (seating 42) in place of a composite coach. This was the only photograph of one of these units submitted for inclusion in this book and it is fortunate that the buffet car is the second vehicle in the train, so can be clearly seen. The location is East Croydon, the unit in view being No.3076 and the picture was taken in February 1968. The train is a rather curious working, the 12.38pm Victoria to East Croydon, apparently a mid-day parcels service that did not convey passengers. A re-organisation of rolling stock resources brought modern 4-CEP/4-BEP stock to the Victoria to Bognor trains in 1964, but 4-BUF units continued in use on many Central Division peak-hour services for some years thereafter. *Chris Evans*

The interior of 4-BUF buffet car No.S12526S, built in 1938 for the Mid-Sussex electrification scheme. This fascinating picture was taken on 2nd May 1970 when the coach was forming part of unit No.3081 on the 12.20pm Portsmouth Harbour to Waterloo train, a route to which the type was moved following a reshuffle of rolling stock. The days of these units were really numbered by then, because replacement 4-CIG/4-BIG stock was starting to become available. These cars contained a kitchen compartment, a bar with ten high, revolving stools and two pairs of peculiarly shaped tables with revolving chairs on each side of the central aisle. There were also two toilet compartments. The interior styling was no doubt considered tasteful at the time of construction, but was probably rather dated by the beginning of the 1950s, never mind the 1970s! After an exhausting day at the office, this hardly seems the most agreeable way to travel home, perched on a stool in the window-less section of one of these cars not noted for their smooth riding characteristics, but after a few whiskies, who cared? *John Hayward*

A further interior illustration of buffet car No.S12526S taken on the same occasion as the previous interior shot. The gentleman in the foreground does not appear to be too impressed by his surroundings, or maybe he was unhappy about the antics of the photographer! Note the most unusual tables adjacent to the windows. The chairs, like the buffet stools, also revolved. These cars offered a total of 26 seats. The door on the left leads into the kitchen compartment, while that on the right is a passenger door. Surely the cups on the counter are not the plastic disposable variety; what a let down for the smartly turned-out attendant in a Pullman uniform! *John Hayward*

The photographer described the unit in this illustration (quite correctly) as a 2-HAL, but the author was delighted to discover that the principal subject is actually No.2700, a unique unit that was only in traffic for a relatively brief period. It was photographed leaving East Croydon at the head of a Victoria to Bognor Regis service, via the Quarry Line and Horsham, on 22nd October 1967. No.2700 was formed in February 1955 from vehicle No.S12664S, an all-steel 82-seat saloon motor coach built in April 1950 and originally allocated to unit No.4590, plus driving trailer composite vehicle No.S12855S. This was one of four accident replacements constructed in late 1954 and these coaches had formica and veneer interior panelling similar to the last batch of 2-HALs, commonly known as the 'Gatwick' units. Rather surprisingly, stencil headcodes were used rather than roller blinds that had largely become standard by this time. No.2700 was disbanded in March 1968, its driving trailer going to 2688 while its motor coach went to 4-SUB unit No.4369. *Chris Gammell*

During the 1950s and 1960s regular summer seaside excursions were operated from London to the South Coast using 4-SUB units, and one of these trains is seen near Star Lane, on the Quarry Line, on 15th September 1963. The leading unit is No.4695, which was one of the very few fitted with a roller blind headcode panel. These excursion trains ran mainly from Victoria or London Bridge, but some started from south London suburban stations such as Tooting and Streatham Hill. Perhaps the most interesting point about these trains, apart from the fact that 4-SUBs were not frequently seen on the Brighton main line, was that twelve-car formations were often booked to provide maximum seating capacity for the day trippers. The lack of toilet facilities may have been an 'inconvenience' on the down journey, but on the return trip must have been an ordeal for many passengers, particularly after a wet afternoon spent in the pub! *R. C. Riley*

Above The Newhaven boat trains will always be particularly associated with the famous 'Brighton' Atlantic steam locomotives that powered them for many years, but by 1967 an electro-diesel locomotive (later Class 73) was the best that could be seen. In this portrait an unidentified member of the class makes a fine sight near Salfords with the evening working to Victoria, which includes a buffet car, on 4th August 1967. The train was subsequently taken over by emu stock, but, despite the fact that Newhaven retains its status as a cross-Channel port, even this no longer runs and the permanent closure of Newhaven Harbour station is reportedly being considered. *John Scrace*

Above left In this delightful wintry scene the 11am Victoria to Brighton, formed of two 5-BEL units in blue and grey livery, rushes out of Quarry tunnel on 8th February 1969. The leading unit is No.3052. There were, of course, three of these units, two of which were booked in traffic while the third was a maintenance 'spare' that worked in rotation with the others. On occasions, and particularly when one of the units was away at Eastleigh for a lengthy heavy repair, a failure might suddenly reduce the fleet to one serviceable set and, rather embarrassingly, a 4-BUF or 4-COR unit would have to be substituted. Needless to say, repair of the defective unit was given top priority and, if necessary, it was rushed up to Selhurst Repair Shop (which has 'lifting' facilities) without delay. There was probably the odd occasion when all three units were 'stopped' for repairs at the same time, no doubt much to the annoyance of the 'Belle's rich and famous patrons. *John Scrace*

Left A Victoria to Littlehampton train, led by 4-CIG unit No.7334 in green livery, races past Salfords some time in late 1969. The North Downs form a distant, hazy backdrop. This was one of the last of the first batch of 4-CIGs – officially known as the Brighton Line replacement stock – to enter service, in early 1966. *Author*

An eight-car Victoria to Littlehampton train approaches Gatwick Airport station on the down fast line some time in the mid-1960s. The leading unit is 4-CIG No.7323, one of 36 constructed at York, together with 18 4-BIG units, to replace the 6-PUL/6-PAN fleet. These four-car sets consist of a driving trailer composite, motor second brake, trailer second open and another driving trailer, which originally provided a total of 42 first and 192 second class seats. It should be borne in mind, however, that in recent years the number of first class seats has generally been reduced with a corresponding increase in the second class accommodation. The lavatories were located solely in the driving trailers. These units represented a major break with 'Southern' traditions, principally because of the adoption of an intermediate non-driving power car, with all four 250hp English Electric traction motors concentrated in one coach. The trailer carriages were mounted on B5(S) type bogies, the first time this design was used on an SR emu, while the motor coaches were equipped with Mk.4 bogies similar to those employed on some 4-CEP units. The 4-CIGs entered public service on 29th March 1965 when a 12-car formation was booked to form the 8.20am Brighton to London Bridge and 5.02pm London Bridge to Eastbourne. At the time of writing these units are still the mainstay of services from London to the Sussex coast and also have many duties in other areas of the former SR. Sadly, in recent years the passenger accommodation of many units has fallen into disrepair and is in disgraceful condition, although it should be said that persistent vandalism is a major problem. *Colour-Rail*

A splendid illustration of Bulleid electric locomotive No.20003 heading down the Brighton Line near Copyhold Junction with a Victoria to Newhaven boat train. This picture was taken on the sunny morning of 17th September 1966, the day that the world famous *Flying Scotsman* steam locomotive made its one, and so far only, visit to Sussex. No.20003, constructed in 1948, was different from its predecessors in many respects, especially the cab ends which were almost flat. These consisted of a central narrow panel flanked by two wider panels that were slightly angled back. This was strikingly similar to the front ends of the production series 4-SUB units, which were being produced in large numbers at the time No.20003 was built. Predictably, sister locomotive Nos. 20001/2, introduced in 1941, had cab ends styled on the first batch of 4-SUBs introduced at the same time. No.20003 was also five tons heavier than the other machines and possessed a higher maximum tractive effort. *Neil Sprinks*

Photographed from a high vantage point near the entrance to Haywards Heath tunnel, the 11am Victoria to Brighton, the first down 'Belle' of the day, passes Haywards Heath on Sunday 27th August 1967. The station here, which is clearly visible in the background, was rebuilt in the early 1930s in the standard Southern Railway style of the period. It consists of two island platforms each capable of accommodating two twelve-coach trains. Note that the goods yard was still in business at that date, but has long since been converted into a huge car park principally for the use of the many commuters who patronise Haywards Heath station. Remarkably, the 'Brighton Belle's formation is not the usual ten-car train, but only nine carriages. Presumably a trailer vehicle was 'stopped' for repair at a time when a spare unit was unavailable. The operating authorities had presumably decided to use the serviceable four-car unit rather than substitute a 4-BUF or 4-COR unit. One wonders if there are many colour pictures of a nine-coach 'Belle'! *John Scrace*

The 9.18am Brighton to London Bridge train is depicted between Hassocks and Burgess Hill on 28th April 1972. The distant South Downs provide an attractive backdrop. Alas, a similar picture is not possible today owing to unrestricted growth of trees on both sides of the tracks. The train is formed of four 2-HAP units which, together with 2-EPB unit Nos. 5651 to 5684, were the last stock to be built by the SR with Bulleid era design features. A total of 36 sets was constructed at Eastleigh Carriage Works using underframes salvaged from withdrawn 2-NOL stock, Nos. 5601 to 5605 appearing in late 1957 while Nos. 5606 to 5636 entered service in 1958. The units consisted of a motor second brake and driving trailer composite providing a total of 18 first and 122 second class seats. The motor coach had two separate saloons, while the composite vehicle had three first and four second class compartments with a side corridor giving access to a toilet located at the inner end of the vehicle. In addition, the latter carriages had a rather grim 'half compartment' seating six persons along a bench seat adjacent to the driver's cab partition. Large single-paned sidelights (windows) were used on the corridor side of the driving trailer and these, together with the Bulleid-style compartment door handles and other interior fittings, gave these vehicles a special character of their own. Early in their careers these units could be found on all three divisions, but in 1972 the entire fleet was allocated to Brighton depot for use on the 'Coastway' services to Hastings and Portsmouth, and they remained at Brighton until displaced by BR-designed 2-HAPs in April 1976. This was the beginning of the end for the fleet; the units were moved to Selhurst, downgraded to 'second class only' and suffered their first withdrawals when the motor coaches from two units were used in No.5263, the prototype refurbishment 4-EPB. Almost all of the remaining units were later disbanded for use in refurbished 4-EPBs, and it is probably true to say they simply faded away, the last three units being withdrawn in May 1983.
John Scrace

Yes, it's the 'Brighton Belle' once again, but who could resist including this really beautiful shot of this famous train, taken at the approach to Clayton tunnel, on the final lap of its journey in April 1968. Unfortunately, by this time the unit's decorative Pullman crests on the front cab sheeting had given way to small yellow panels, but even so the train looks very smart and particularly inviting with the table lamps (two of which are just visible) giving the coaches a very cosy atmosphere. *Gerald Daniels*

Right This picture hardly requires explanation! Here, the name 'Mona' is displayed on the side of the coach at Brighton station in 1969, this car being formed in unit No.3053. Many regular passengers had a special affection for the 'Belle', so no wonder there was uproar when BR pronounced that the train was to be withdrawn. *John Hayward*

The interiors of the second class Pullman cars were certainly not as roomy as the first class version, but even so were very attractive and reasonably luxurious. Here, we take a peep inside car No.85 which was allocated to 'Brighton Belle' unit No.3053. This view was recorded at Brighton station on 2nd March 1969. The formation of this unit was second class cars Nos. 93 & 85, first class cars 'Mona' and 'Gwen' and second class car No.92. During the Second World War, Pullman, buffet and pantry facilities were withdrawn from 22nd May 1942, the Pullman cars being stored out of use. Unit No.3053 returned to traffic in November 1946. *John Hayward*

Pictured in lovely spring sunshine, the 10.28am Victoria to Brighton semi-fast train approaches Clayton tunnel, between Hassocks and Preston Park stations, on the morning of 16th March 1968. The leading unit is 4-LAV No.2933 while the other coaches appear to be two 2-BIL units. The year 1968 saw the condemnation of many 4-LAVs, including unit No.2933, as replacement 4-VEPs became available, and the final 4-LAV workings took place in February 1969 when the type passed into history. *Gerald Daniels*

In this picture, taken at Preston Park station in April 1968, 4-LAV unit No.2924 is depicted pulling away from the up through platform with the 10.28am Brighton to Victoria service. At that time there were 'fast', 'semi-fast' and 'stopping' Brighton to Victoria services, and this would have been known to operating staff as a 'stopping' or 'slow' train. It was 'slow' in every sense of the word, stopping at every station as far as Purley (via Redhill), and then would have called at East Croydon and Clapham Junction before reaching Victoria at 12.07pm, an exhilarating (!) total journey time of 1 hour 39 min. One wonders how many passengers turned up at Brighton station and just boarded the first Victoria train timetabled, later to find themselves suffering the indignity of being overtaken by virtually every other train on the Brighton Line! At one time there were berthing sidings at Preston Park, with three roads each accommodating twelve cars, and the front ends of (presumably) a 4-CIG and 4-COR can just be discerned in the background. Most of the trackwork is still there at the time of writing, but is very overgrown and has become an eyesore, however there are plans to reinstate two sidings at this location. *Gerald Daniels*

Even in the best regulated industries accidents can sometimes happen and in this shot taken at Brighton, Lovers Walk, depot on 23rd June 1968, two units have suffered in a shunting mishap or, in railwayman's parlance, 'a minor pitch-in'. The blue/grey unit, 4-BIG No.7033, does not seem to be too badly affected, but the wooden-bodied driving trailer coach of 2-BIL No.2096 appears to be a 'write off'. The latter coach was later condemned and replaced with a similar vehicle from No.2010, one of the original units with detail differences. No.2096 subsequently survived for only a short time, however, and was withdrawn in 1969. Notice the incredible array of other rolling stock visible in the photograph. Apart from the remarkable variety of emu liveries on display, the Top Yard, on the other side of the main line tracks, appears to be busy with a diesel shunter on duty. How much more interesting the railway was even at that (comparatively recent) time compared to the dull uniformity of today! Beyond London Road viaduct (note the 'new' section built following war damage) hundreds of rooftops provide a distinctive background. The cluster of large buildings on the horizon is Brighton General Hospital. *Colour-Rail*

The Chief Mechanical & Electrical Engineer's instruction unit No.053 is depicted at Brighton station during an enthusiasts' special event on 30th June 1973. Steam locomotives from the National Collection, which were housed in the former Preston Park Pullman works at that time, can just be glimpsed in the background. This unit, originally No.S10S, was formed in 1956 and the coaches were numbered DS40 to DS42. These had been respectively Nos. 8564, 9658 and 9817, formerly LSWR steam carriages that were converted to electric operation and entered service as 3-SUB unit No.1782 in 1931. This unit was later augmented to run as a 4-SUB and renumbered 4579. No.053 contained a lecture and projection room, plus a display of brake, power control and heating and lighting equipment. This unique survivor was normally hidden from view in depot sidings, this shot being taken at one of its rare public appearances. *David Wigley*

The end of the 6-PUL units was commemorated by a rail tour organised by the Locomotive Club of Great Britain and in this portrait unit No.3041 is seen amidst the unmistakable surroundings of Brighton station on 24th April 1966. This unit was originally one of three sets (classified 6-CIT) built primarily for use on business services between London Bridge and Brighton which were largely patronised by first class ticket holders. The set numbers were 2041 to 2043 (3041 to 3043 from January 1937). These units were similar to the 6-PULs, but the three ordinary trailer coaches were seven-compartment first class vehicles, rather than composites. Seating was provided for 138 first and 124 third class passengers. The coach nearest to the camera, No.S11001S, is especially interesting, being built by BRCW Co. in late 1931 as an experimental vehicle with a straight bodyside profile, this being usual 'Southern' practice at the time. Note the deep panelling completely covering the solebar, a very unusual design feature for 'Southern' stock. Another experimental coach, No.S11002S, was constructed with curved sides and this design was subsequently adopted for the 6-PUL fleet. These vehicles were tested on the Brighton Line using a five-car rake of converted steam stock, which must have been a weird sight! After the Second World War the first class only coaches were converted to either composites or

third class and the units reclassified 6-PUL. After this special run, No.3041 was reformed as a 6-COR unit, losing its Pullman car in the process. It remained in traffic in this guise for a further three years, mainly employed on South Eastern Division peak-hour commuter workings, Saturday seaside 'extras', and relief boat trains. *John Hayward*

Right A close-up of the Pullman coat of arms visible above the doorway in the picture below. First class and composite cars were given distinguishing names while second class vehicles were merely numbered. *John Hayward*

Remarkably spacious seating with plushly upholstered armchairs, a lamp on every table giving a cosy, intimate atmosphere and absolutely splendid marquetry work on the wooden panels adorning the bulkheads ... there was certainly something very special about Pullman travel. In addition, of course, there was always the delightful smell of freshly prepared meals wafting along from the kitchens, which no photograph could ever convey. In this picture the first class section of Pullman car 'Alice' is portrayed and this shot was also taken on 24th April 1966, when it was marshalled in unit No.3041. When new 'Alice' was formed in unit No.2009 (later renumbered 3009), so it had obviously been reformed at some stage. *John Hayward*

Cliffe Hill, in the background, and the distinctive station layout provide immediate clues to the location of this picture which is, of course, Lewes. 4-COR unit No.3102 is seen entering the station with an eastbound working from Brighton in the early 1970s, while 4-COR unit No.3109 is berthed in a siding on the right. Passengers on the coastal routes radiating from Brighton sometimes had to tolerate units in poor condition approaching withdrawal, the 2-BIL/2-HAL units being in that category. The 4-CORs also finished their working lives on the coastal lines, being replaced in the autumn of 1972 by Southern Railway-designed 2-HAP stock, which few passengers probably considered to be an improvement. *Author*

The East Coast Line

In this attractive picture 4-COR unit No.3143 is seen leaving Berwick station with an Eastbourne to Brighton service on 8th April 1972. The modest, rural station there is probably one of the most isolated featured in this book, the hamlet of Berwick being more than a mile away, while the nearest settlement of any importance is Alfriston, over two miles distant. This scene has not changed much since this shot was taken, the signal box (which can just be discerned) is still there at the time of writing as are the semaphore signals and, of course, the South Downs on the far horizon. No.3143 was built in early 1938 for the Mid-Sussex electrification, but by the time of this picture it was approaching the end of its career, and was subsequently broken-up for scrap. *John Scrace*

Left Looking decidedly lost in the magnificent downland landscape east of Lewes, a solitary 2-BIL unit passes over Southerham Junction and crosses the River Ouse as it approaches Lewes East Junction signal box with an unidentified up local train on 19th March 1967. Cliffe Hill, which rises to a height of 538ft above sea level, once again dominates the background. In the author's opinion this was one of the best, possibly *the* best, photographic spots in Sussex but, alas, it has since been ruined by a road scheme and industrial development alongside the river. Part of the former Eastwoods cement works is just visible on the extreme right of the shot. *Gerald Daniels*

The Victorian villas of Hastings provide a distinctive background to this illustration of 4-COR unit No.3116 leaving with the 6.11pm to Brighton on 15th July 1972, just a few months before these characterful units bowed out. The track layout and signalling at this end of Hastings station has been considerably altered since this shot was taken. The semaphores have been replaced by colour light signals (semaphores are still *in situ* at the eastern end of the station at the time of writing) and the up loop platform, adjacent to where the diesel unit is standing, has been converted into a bay for the use of Hastings to Ashford diesel services. *Michael Allen*

A portrait of a forgotten station. At one time Ore station, serving a substantial residential neighbourhood on the eastern fringe of Hastings, was the starting point of regular services to London Victoria and Brighton and was additionally served by local diesel trains running across the marshes to Ashford. There was also a rolling stock berthing shed, so Ore, the limit of the electrified area east of Hastings, was a fairly important location. But, since this photograph of unit No.3154 forming the 3.14pm to Brighton was taken on 27th August 1972, there has been a marked decline in the station's status. All of the buildings seen here have been demolished, the berthing depot suffered the same fate after years of dereliction, and, even worse, Ore's train service has been drastically curtailed. Electric services to London Victoria and Brighton now start from Hastings, the only through London trains being confined to a few weekday rush-hour workings to Charing Cross. It is strange that a station in such a densely populated area is not considered to have any significant traffic potential; perhaps the passengers would return if a reasonable service was provided. *Chris Evans*

The Mid-Sussex Line

The line between Horsham and Arundel is, at least in the author's opinion, one of the most attractive in Sussex with mile after mile of unspoilt scenery, particularly south of Pulborough. The view of the castle from the window of a train approaching Arundel is certainly one of the most memorable in the south of England. Unfortunately, despite being one of the prettiest routes covered in this album, the Mid-Sussex Line (as it used to be known) is also one of the least photographed, presumably due to its early electrification and relatively sparse service which ensured it was always overshadowed by the Brighton Line. In this picture, taken in August 1969, a Victoria to Bognor Regis service is seen heading down the valley towards Arundel with the river Arun just in the shot on the right. The train is formed of two 2-BIL units, with a 2-HAL unit on the rear. Today, the geographically incorrect and very misleading 'Mid-Sussex' title has been replaced by the 'Arun Valley Line'.
Author

The graceful curve of Brighton station's roof above the West Coast Line platforms immediately identifies the location of this photograph. The magnificent roof, being a listed structure, cannot be demolished and many enthusiasts would probably wish that similar status had been conferred on 4-COR unit No.3129 standing in Platform 2 with a local working on 8th April 1972. If so, it would probably still be around today! Alas, like all of its remaining sister units, No.3129 was in its final year of service and condemned during the autumn of that year. It was the last of 29 units built in the first half of 1937 for the Portsmouth Direct Line electrification. *Michael Allen*

The West Coast Line

Virtually everything of railway interest in this photograph taken at Littlehampton station on 8th April 1972 has since been consigned to the history books. 4-COR unit No.3158 was destined not to survive beyond the end of the summer 1972 timetable, while the station itself was later completely rebuilt, the old, somewhat neglected platform canopies being demolished in the process. Incredibly, the ancient 'Brighton' steam locomotive shed, the top of which is just visible above the left-hand canopy, survived the onslaught and is still standing at the time of writing. Unit No.3158 had a particularly fascinating history, as it was one of three additional 4-CORs (Nos.3156 to 3158) made-up in place of three disbanded 4-RES units after the Second World War. It incorporated a unique trailer composite, No.S11861S, which was formerly 4-RES trailer dining first No.S12232S. This had apparently been modified internally during the war, the former first class dining area being converted into a third class saloon. No.3158 ran with this 'odd' vehicle, which had eight seats less than a normal composite, until March 1964 when the opportunity arose to substitute coach No.S11861S with a standard trailer composite coach, No.S11824S. *Michael Allen*

This wonderfully evocative picture recalls memories of the long period when virtually everything on the SR was painted in either regional cream or green paint, the latter colour being particularly prominent in this shot! The location is Barnham and a Portsmouth Harbour to Brighton semi-fast train, with 2-BIL unit No.2051 leading, is seen awaiting departure on 1st March 1969. At this time there were hourly semi-fast and all-stations trains between those places, but only the latter currently survive, the semi-fast services being replaced in part by the comparatively new Victoria to Southampton trains via Hove. Note the 'sausage' station signs and various items of station furniture, including a rather unsightly dustbin on the right. Presumably the railway's 'image' was not so important at that time. *John Hayward*

Photographed against the rather depressing background of the remains of the goods yard, 2-BIL unit No.2016 is depicted leading a Portsmouth Harbour to Brighton stopping train away from Havant on 26th June 1971, shortly before this stock was eliminated. This unit was the oldest of its type in service when the last surviving sets were withdrawn just over a month after this shot was taken. The rear unit is an unidentified 2-HAL. At one time three tracks crossed the roadway at this point and, judging by the new road surface, the headshunt for the goods yard had only recently been removed. A small section of the abandoned Hayling Island branch can just be seen behind the signal box. Since this scene was recorded the up fast line through the station, and the just visible rusty connection from the up loop line towards Hayling Island, have been removed. *David Wigley*

Lewes to Haywards Heath

The South Downs, on the distant horizon, form the backdrop as 6-PUL unit No.3010 leads an Ore to Victoria twelve-car formation northwards near Cooksbridge on 13th June 1965. The writing was on the wall for these units by this date because the first 4-CIGs were already in traffic and the old 6-PUL/6-PAN stock was being progressively withdrawn. This shot was the only picture of an electric train on the Lewes to Haywards Heath section submitted for inclusion in this album, and it is more than likely that the photographer took it to 'pass the time' while he was waiting to photograph a steam-hauled railtour. *Graham Hoare*

In late 1958 the 4-CEP units earmarked for use on Phase One of the Kent Coast electrification scheme started to be delivered, and had to be stored until the new electric service was introduced in June 1959. The new units were stabled at various locations, including Ford, Barnham and Gatwick on the Central Division, there presumably being no spare berthing capacity available on the South Eastern Division. A small number of 2-HAPs also appeared at some of these points. In early 1959 it was decided to concentrate the 4-CEP units on the Haywards Heath to Horsted Keynes branch, which only had an hourly passenger service, thus enabling one running line to be used for storage purposes, while the other track was converted for single line working. The first 4-CEP units reportedly appeared on the branch on about 7th February 1959, stored on the former down line. In order to prevent the units from 'seizing up' two train crews were regularly booked to move the stock. One crew would take a 12-car rake from the front of the queue on a run to Seaford or Eastbourne while the other crew would have the less interesting task of moving the other units down the line. Unit No.7128 is the nearest to the camera in this shot taken near Ardingly station on 17th May 1959. *R. C. Riley*

The Horsted Keynes Branch

A further view of the long line of stored 4-CEP units near Ardingly station on 17th May 1959, looking towards Horsted Keynes. Motor coach No.S61340 was originally formed in unit No.7129 which became set No.1513 following refurbishment at Swindon Works. Note that even lowly second class passengers had the benefit of curtains in those days to reduce cold draughts in the winter-time and protect them from the glare of the sun in the summer. It seems amazing that the railway authorities were able to store these units safely in this way, apparently without fear of youths causing damage. Today, such a move could not be contemplated, because stored rolling stock is a very tempting target for graffiti-spraying vandals and arsonists so has to be protected. *R. C. Riley*

'Horsted Keynes – Alight Here For The Bluebell Line'. It may not be immediately apparent, but this picture is of considerable historical significance because it was taken during the relatively short period when it was possible to change there onto a Bluebell train. The Bluebell was not permitted to run into Horsted Keynes station until 29th October 1961 when it linked up with the BR system for the first time. During 1962 regular connections were made between BR and Bluebell services and the latter probably hoped this development would save the Horsted Keynes branch from closure. Alas, it was not to be, and the branch was closed on 27th October 1963, by an unfortunate coincidence almost exactly two years after the Bluebell's triumphant entry to Horsted Keynes station. In this portrait 2-HAL unit No.2662, accompanied by a 2-BIL unit, stands at Horsted Keynes on a wet and gloomy day in 1962. A four-coach formation was something of a luxury on the branch as two cars were usually more than enough for the meagre amount of traffic on offer. *John Edgington*

Central Suburban

Sunshine with a sprinkling of snow on the ground, the kind of conditions that railway photographers dream of! Most of them would probably prefer a steam locomotive emitting clouds of smoke and steam but, alas, by the date of this photograph the SR had consigned steam traction to history and the photographer had to make do with an uninspiring 4-EPB. What a pity! Unit No.5012, seen here leaving Forest Hill station with a southbound local working, still manages to create an interesting scene as it passes a typical Southern Railway-style brick-built signal box on 8th February 1969. At the time of the picture 4-EPBs were very much an everyday sight at Forest Hill but, just like steam traction, they have disappeared from the scene, while the signal box was superseded by London Bridge power box. *Chris Gammell*

Yes, another picture of a 4-SUB fitted with a roller blind route indicator! No.4700, illustrated here leaving Sydenham whilst forming the 5.23pm London Bridge to Coulsdon North semi-fast train on 28th May 1975, was one of only a handful of these units fitted in the 1960s with roller blind route indicators in place of the stencil plate type. This was, perhaps, surprising in view of the fact that all of the 4-CORs were so modified, even though most units were at least a decade older and did not require such frequent changing of the route display! Incredibly, despite there being only ten 4-SUB units equipped in this way, there were at least three different variations of headcode panel and unit No.4660, for example, had a headcode box which protruded considerably from the cab panelling. Two units, reportedly Nos. 4355 and 4736, only had roller blinds at one end! *Chris Evans*

West Croydon station is the unmistakable setting for this picture of 4-SUB unit No.4107 departing with a Victoria to Epsom Downs train on 5th June 1966. The steam train, just visible on the left of the shot, is the 'Surrey Rambler' railtour which was reversing there. The materials for the construction of the first ten 4-SUBs were reported to be available before the outbreak of the Second World War in September 1939, but the work was suspended due to the start of hostilities, and the first of the new units, No.4101, was not added to operational stock until October 1941. Unit No.4107 entered service in February 1945. The accommodation in unit Nos. 4101 to 4110 was all in compartments, the motor coaches having nine, while there were eleven compartments in one of the trailers, the other having only ten. This was because one of the trailer vehicles was designed to be a composite coach, the two compartments at each end being third class while the remainder were designated first. A decision was taken, however, to withdraw first class

accommodation from London suburban trains from 6th October 1941. Subsequent units had their first class compartments finished as third. These units provided seats for no fewer than 468 passengers, but they were notoriously cramped with very narrow compartments and, therefore, unpopular with passengers. Perhaps the most interesting aspect of this stock was its steel body construction, using steel framing and panelling. The driving cabs were also made of all-welded steel, including the domed roof. The principal section of the roof was traditional wood and canvas, however, and the 'join' between the roof and steel bodysides is clearly visible in the photograph. These distinctive units, besides being the oldest, also had (what had become by the early 1970s) non-standard 339-type traction motors, and were the first 4-SUBs to be phased out. No.4107 was one of the last of this type, surviving until May 1972. *John Hayward*

A Wimbledon to West Croydon train, formed of BR Standard 2-EPB 'Tyneside' unit No.5792, rounds the curve past Wandle Park and approaches West Croydon station on 28th March 1965. This unit was one of 15 built at Eastleigh Carriage Works in 1954/55 for use on the Newcastle Central to South Shields route, where the first unit entered public service on 11th February 1955. Passenger accommodation in the motor coach consisted of two semi-saloons seating 74 persons, ten fewer than the equivalent SR units due to the larger brake van on the Tyneside stock. The driving trailer composite vehicles originally had 90 third and eight first class seats, with the passenger accommodation comprising of one saloon of four seating bays, followed by five separate compartments with that adjacent to the saloon being designated first class. First class was, however, abolished on the Tyneside electrics in May 1959. An especially fascinating feature of the stock, apart from the

fact that no unit numbers were carried, was the headcode panel consisting of four headlamps. In normal passenger service the top two lamps were illuminated. The South Shields line was dieselised from 7th January 1963 and the units, which were still relatively modern, moved south arriving later the same month. All of the units received full overhauls and required considerable modification before entering service on the SR. They were classified 2-EPB and numbered 5781 to 5795. At first the 'new' stock could be found anywhere on the Central and South Eastern divisions, but in July 1974 it was moved *en masse* to East Wimbledon depot. The first withdrawals took place in May 1984 and five months later all of the remaining units were taken out of traffic apparently due to their 'non-standard' bogies. Some units remained stored out of use for a long time after withdrawal and were subsequently converted for departmental use. *Colour-Rail*

A view of the London end of Sutton station on 13th November 1975 showing 4-SUB unit No.4277 running in with the 12.06pm Victoria to Dorking train. Sutton is a very busy outer-suburban station, but still retained semaphore signalling when this picture was taken; the delightful semaphores were replaced when the Victoria signalling centre was commissioned. The rattling 4-SUBs were part of the scene for so long that enthusiasts (and passengers, of course!) probably thought they would go on for ever. They certainly offered much more comfortable seating than the Class 455 replacements, even if their riding was not quite as good, and were simple, reliable units. No.4277 achieved a degree of fame when it was used on the 8.16am from Waterloo via the Kingston Loop on 11th July 1983, this train reportedly being the final booked 4-SUB working on the South Western Division. The last 4-SUBs were taken out of traffic without ceremony on 6th September 1983, the unit depicted here being one of the final survivors. *Chris Evans*

Maunsell 4-SUB unit No.4306 poses with an unknown all-steel unit in September 1958; the location is clearly apparent from the photograph! This unit first saw the light of day in the spring of 1925 as 3-car set No.1291 and was built for use on the Waterloo to Guildford via Cobham service. A total of 26 sets was constructed, numbered 1285 to 1310. The motor coaches were built by the Metropolitan Carriage Wagon & Finance Co. Ltd, and the trailers by the Midland Railway Carriage & Wagon Co. Ltd. Metropolitan Vickers Ltd provided the electrical equipment. The motor coaches had seven third class compartments and weighed 39 tons while the trailer coach (27 tons) had six first class compartments and three thirds, with the former being in the middle of the vehicles. The total length of the units was 181ft 8ins overall, it being interesting to note that the trailer vehicles were three feet longer than the motor coaches. The bodies were constructed of teak with steel panelling and the units perpetuated an updated version of an earlier LSWR design feature, the distinctive wedge- (or bow-) ended cab front which certainly made them look 'different'. In the mid-1940s the units were augmented by 28-ton ten-compartment trailer thirds, which increased the units' length to 245ft and boosted the seating capacity to 380 third class passengers (first class on suburban trains had been abolished by that time). These units were ousted by new BR Standard 4-EPB stock in the early 1960s. *John Edgington*

A vintage scene at Tulse Hill, taken in the late 1950s, depicting 4-SUB unit No.4551 leaving the station with (what appears to be) a West Croydon to Holborn Viaduct service via Sutton and Wimbledon. The tracks in the foreground are those to London Bridge via Peckham Rye. Note the signal, apparently installed on a former a.c. overhead electrification gantry. No.4551 was formerly a LBSCR a.c. three-set which was converted to d.c. unit No.1754 in January 1930 for use on various newly-electrified suburban routes. It consisted of an eight-compartment motor third brake, a composite trailer with six third and four first class compartments and a motor composite brake. The latter had three first and four third class compartments. The overall length of the unit was 193ft 5ins and the weight 104 tons, the electrical equipment being supplied by Metropolitan Vickers. In the late 1940s No.1754 was converted to a four-coach set by the addition of all-steel trailer No.S10453S and renumbered 4551. Later its LBSCR trailer vehicle was replaced by a former LSWR coach previously marshalled in unit No.4574. Like others of this type, No.4551 ended its days in the late 1950s, but its all-steel trailer, which was of much more recent construction, survived to run as part of 4-EPB No.5249 and was later refurbished, becoming part of unit No.5434. *R. C. Riley*

The former LNWR/LMSR Knights Hill coal depot, between Tulse Hill and North Dulwich, may be a strange location for a picture of an SR emu, but that was where de-icing unit No.S95 was photographed on 14th September 1960. The unit had been hauled there by a steam locomotive and is seen standing on the now demolished Rosendale Road bridge, awaiting entry to Peckham Rye depot for attention. The coaches seen here were originally built in 1925 and allocated to three-car set No.1514, which was converted to a four-car unit in 1946 by the insertion of an all-steel trailer coach and renumbered 4344. Withdrawal and conversion of the motor coaches for de-icing purposes occurred in 1960 and the vehicles became Nos. ADS 70094/95. Set No.95 was renumbered 014 in 1968 and was eventually withdrawn in 1979. *R. C. Riley*

South Eastern Division

The electric train with the highest profile on the South Eastern Division was undoubtedly the 'Golden Arrow', and many people would argue that it was the most famous electrically-hauled working on BR. The 'Golden Arrow' was inaugurated on 15th May 1929, but patronage of the pre-war train was not up to expectations, largely due to the depressed state of the world economy. It ceased operation during the Second World War, but was reintroduced on 15th April 1946, leaving London at 10am and arriving in Paris at 6.45pm. During the ensuing years numerous changes were made to the timings, both to stimulate more business and compete with the increasing threat from the airlines. Unfortunately, the railways could never match the speed and convenience offered by the airlines and the 'Arrow' was soon on a downward spiral. It must have been sad for regular travellers to witness its steady decline from a BR flagship service to an almost anonymous boat train conveying a token complement of Pullman Cars marshalled on the rear of a rake of Mk.1 coaches. In this June 1968 picture No.E5011 at the head of the train looks smart enough, with its headboard and flags prominent, but the rest of the stock hardly conjures up much of the old glory for which the train was so famous. The 'Golden Arrow' disappeared from the timetables in 1972, but today, due to the opening of the Channel Tunnel, for many people rail is once again the preferred option for travel to Paris. *Ken Wightman*

Charing Cross to Dover

Electro-diesel locomotive No.E6006, seen here posing at Hither Green shed on 8th June 1963, was one of six machines built at Eastleigh Carriage Works in 1962. They were extremely versatile, being able to work as an ordinary electric locomotive taking current from the third rail, or as a diesel-electric when used for shunting and freight working over non-electrified lines. They were equipped with four English Electric 400hp traction motors giving a total of 1,600hp when working on electrified routes. On non-electrified lines a diesel generator powered the motors, though the output was reduced to 600hp. When working on the third rail, the locomotives were intended to work freight trains of 700 tons up a gradient of 1 in 70 and passenger trains of up to ten coaches. The locomotives were 53ft 8ins long, weighed 75 tons, and were fitted to work with rolling stock equipped with electro-pneumatic and vacuum brakes. When the locomotives were built it was intended that they would run in multiple with other locomotives and units with compatible control and braking systems, and in the early 1960s trials took place in Kent with 4-CEP units. In later years, however, in practice only the main batch of 'small' electro-diesel locomotives, built in 1966/67 by English Electric at Vulcan Works, Newton-le-Willows, Lancashire, were used in multiple with other locomotives and units, the first series being banned apparently due to their slightly non-standard electrical equipment. It should be mentioned, however, that the earlier machines were able to operate in multiple with each other. This design was a great success, and at the time of writing a handful of these locomotives remain in operation more than forty years after their introduction, their duties including working Victoria to Gatwick Airport services. *Colin Caddy*

When electric locomotives Nos. E5000 to E5012 were built at Doncaster Works for Phase One of the Kent Coast electrification in 1959 (a further batch was constructed later) they were fitted with pantographs, in addition to shoes for current collection from the third rail. This was to enable their use in freight yards, such as Dover, Faversham and Hoo Junction, where live rails would have been a safety hazard for staff. The decline in railway freight traffic, plus the use of other types of traction, presumably made the pantographs redundant and a decision was made to take them out of use. This rare picture of one of these machines with its pantograph raised was taken on the last day that they were operational, 25th September 1976, and depicts No.71 001 demonstrating this equipment in Hither Green yard. All of these locomotives were withdrawn by the end of 1978, so were extremely short-lived, particularly when compared to other rolling stock introduced on the Kentish lines at the same time, some of which survived into the 21st century! This locomotive has since been preserved as part of the National Collection. *R. C. Riley*

The classic photographic position just south of Polhill tunnel has long been a favourite with generations of railway photographers, and in this scene a train of empty stock from Stewarts Lane to either Dover or Folkestone is illustrated running downhill towards Dunton Green in August 1973. Unfortunately, headcode No.10 applied both to Dover and Folkestone-bound empty trains from Stewarts Lane depot, so the destination of this working will always be a mystery. The leading unit is 4-CEP No.7132 and the train is made up of a 4-BEP, in the middle, and another 4-CEP, which was very much the usual formation of boat trains at this time. Note that there is one other vehicle visible at the rear of the train, possibly a motor luggage van (MLV) or one of the short-lived trailer luggage vans (TLV). If it was the latter it would have been accompanied by an MLV because the TLVs, which were BR Standard full brake coaches modified for use with SR emu stock, did not have driving cabs so had to be formed intermediately. The TLVs were introduced in 1968, but only lasted until 1975, reportedly due to their unpopularity with operating staff. *Ken Smith*

In this mid-1960s view a Margate to Charing Cross train, led by 4-CEP unit No.7182, passes Tonbridge station on the up through line. The 25 miles-long straight section of line from Ashford ends abruptly at Tonbridge where there is a notoriously tight curve for trains on the London route at the west end of the station. This has been realigned many times in order to ease the severe permanent speed restrictions at this point. The scene shown here has not changed greatly over the years, the station retains its Southern Railway style platform awnings and, at the time of writing, it is still possible to observe 4-CEP units. The widespread introduction of new stock is rapidly reducing the activities of the 4-CEPs, however, and it is possible that they will have disappeared from the scene by the time this book appears in print. They have served Kent for more than 40 years: what better tribute could they have? *Colour-Rail*

During the period covered by this volume there were around one hundred 4-CEP units operating in Kent, so it seems remarkable that three of the small number of transparencies submitted for inclusion in this album featured unit No.7182. What was it about this particular unit that made it such an irresistible attraction for photographers? Well, here is No.7182 once again, this time heading a test train of three 4-CEP units through Ashford station in the spring of 1961 past a group of onlookers on the down platform. At this time Ashford station still had all the atmosphere of the steam age, the smoke-blackened overbridge, semaphore signals, a water crane and even an engineman admiring the new stock as it passed by. Today, Ashford boasts international Eurostar services and the station has been totally rebuilt – for the second time in forty years (!) – to cater for these trains. The contrast could not be more marked. *Gerald Daniels*

A lot of criticism was directed at BR's corporate livery, introduced in 1965, but here is one type that looked reasonably attractive in blue, at least prior to the painting of full yellow ends. Judging by the immaculate condition of its running gear, electro-diesel locomotive No.E6029 was clearly brand new when pictured at Folkestone Harbour station in April 1966. It certainly looks very smart with its white cab window surrounds and roof. One wonders how long the gleaming white roof panels remained in such pristine condition! The red blinds and tail lamp suggest that it is about to assist a train up the hill to Folkestone Junction. Unfortunately, the identity of this train is unknown; maybe it was a special. *Ken Wightman*

The white cliffs of Dover, one of Great Britain's most familiar landmarks, have provided thousands of cross-channel passengers with their first glimpse of the British mainland, and doubtless one of their most enduring memories. Here, a tiny part of the cliffs is visible on the left, providing a memorable backdrop to this picture of the 11.23am Ramsgate to Charing Cross train. The units are 4-CEP Nos 7201 and 7157 and this picture was taken on Christmas Eve 1975. The cliffs have overlooked railway operations here for over 150 years, and until quite recently Dover was bustling with both passenger and freight traffic bound for the continent. There was a substantial freight yard, locomotive shed in steam days and, of course, Dover Marine station (later Western Docks) which was mostly dedicated to boat train traffic. Alas, Dover's importance as a cross-channel port for railway traffic has declined dramatically since the opening of the Channel Tunnel and most of the railway installations overlooked by the cliffs have been largely abandoned. *Chris Evans*

When the Kent coast lines were electrified it was decided to use multiple units for nearly all boat trains, these being much more flexible operationally than loco-hauled formations, a distinct advantage at Folkestone where reversal was required. Even though a 12-car rake of 4-CEP stock had six luggage compartments, this was deemed to be insufficient bearing in mind the huge amounts of luggage conveyed on boat trains. The conversion of some BR Standard full brake vehicles was considered (six were converted in 1968), but this option was ruled out at the time because it would have made the trains slightly under-powered. The SR opted for motored vans, these having the added advantage that they could be used on their own for other duties, such as parcels workings. Eastleigh had already produced a vehicle of this type, No.E68000, for the South Tyneside line in 1955. This had its guards' accommodation sandwiched between the two luggage compartments, but on the vans built for the SR it was located at one end of the vehicle and gave access to the driving cab. Entry to the other cab was via a vestibule. The vans built for the SR, numbered S68001 to S68010, were extremely versatile, being equipped with batteries enabling them to work in non-electrified sidings and onto quays. No.S68006 is depicted on the quay at Dover Marine on 12th May 1961. The batteries were charged from a motor generator set when the vehicle was running on the third rail. Another advantage was the vans' vacuum brake facility which meant they could be used to haul short parcels trains of up to 100 tons gross, and they reportedly had a regular working to Redhill for a time. These vehicles rarely had a high profile, but in many ways were one of the most interesting types to operate on the SR's electrified system in recent years.
John Langford

Dover Priory station's cramped location between two tunnels hardly made it a favourite spot for railway photographers, not that many, judging by the shortage of pictures of electric stock in this area, seem to have ventured to this part of Kent. Even when the sun was shining at Dover Priory there were problems with deep shadows, as illustrated here. This view was taken in August 1969 and depicts 4-CEP No.7194, a unit apparently well overdue for shops as indicated by its appallingly discoloured paintwork. The damage was usually caused by the carriage cleaning fluid, used in carriage washing machines, being insufficiently washed off after each application and after a while the paintwork became badly stained. *Author*

Most enthusiasts have observed Stewarts Lane depot, and the maze of tracks surrounding it, from the windows of a train passing above the site on a viaduct, so this view, taken from ground level, may be slightly novel. It shows immaculate 4-BEP unit No.7010 returning to the depot after working a Royal train on 18th July 1975. The unit was presumably just 'ex-works', hence its selection for such a prestigious duty. The tracks on the left used to serve part of the old steam shed. No.7010 was built for Phase One of the Kent Coast electrification scheme and was completed in May 1959. It consisted of two motor second brake coaches, each seating 56 passengers, a corridor composite coach with 24 first and second class seats, plus a buffet car. The latter vehicle had a quite spacious kitchen, plus a bar, while seats for 21 passengers were provided. No.7010 was later refurbished at Swindon Works, becoming 4-CEP No.1534, but it should be noted that its buffet car was replaced by a BR Mk.1 coach which was also refurbished. *Chris Evans*

Victoria to Ramsgate

A rare view of the SR General Manager's saloon inside Stewarts Lane inspection shed on 18th July 1975. This coach is a clever conversion of Hastings-gauge buffet car No.S60755, which was withdrawn from passenger use in January 1964 following a reduction of catering facilities on the route. The narrow, straight-sided body profile is clearly apparent in the picture. Irreverently known to lesser SR staff as the 'gin palace', the saloon was assigned for the personal use of the General Manager, his staff and other officials from the BRB hierarchy. The coach was extensively altered, most of the kitchen and dining areas being converted into two separate saloons which were used for 'on site' meetings. Part of the kitchen and the staff toilet were retained. The saloon was designed for maximum operational flexibility, being fitted with side buffers, a central rubbing plate and drophead buckeye couplings and this equipment, together with the necessary electrical modifications, enabled the coach to operate in multiple with a wide range of SR emu stock and locomotives. Drivers' controls were fitted at both ends. The vehicle was mounted on standard B5(S) bogies, one of which was fitted with retractable shoegear. The saloon's accommodation was quite luxurious and occasionally it was employed on VIP specials. In 1981 it was used to convey HRH The Prince of Wales, and his late wife Diana, to Romsey for their honeymoon. The following year it was provided when the Pope travelled from Gatwick Airport to Victoria. *Chris Evans*

The incomparable 'Golden Arrow' was undoubtedly one of Great Britain's most famous expresses and, in steam days, was especially noted for the immaculate condition of the locomotive and Pullman carriages that formed the train. In June 1961 electric traction took over from steam, using 2,552hp Doncaster-built Bo-Bos, later known as Class 71. During the 1960s the fortunes of the 'Arrow' declined, and by the time this picture of the train approaching Shortlands was taken in the summer of 1968 the train was mostly composed of 'ordinary' Mk.1 vehicles and, indeed, there is not a Pullman car to be seen! The locomotive, No.E5004, hardly looks its best in corporate blue with a ghastly all-over yellow front end. Whatever had happened to the old pride, magic and mystique of this splendid train? *Ken Wightman*

'British Rail regret that owing to a train failure in the Shortlands area, all services will be subject to delay or cancellation'. It is not clear precisely what is happening here, but it appears that the electric locomotive hauling the 'Golden Arrow' expired approaching Shortlands station and required the assistance of a following 12-coach Victoria to Ramsgate train, thus producing a massive 22-coach cavalcade. Let us hope that the passengers aboard the 'Arrow' did not miss their boat! This photograph, which was taken on 26th March 1967, shows the train's formation at this time, which included a token complement of only four Pullman cars. The photographer, the late Ken Wightman, lived in a house which backed onto the railway at this point, so he was ideally placed to record this interesting scene.

When BR announced the modernisation of the Kent Coast services their plans naturally included new electric rolling stock to operate the trains. It must have come as something as a shock to passengers, therefore, when ten 6-COR units, formed of redundant Brighton Line 6-PUL/6-PAN stock built in the early 1930s, were later drafted onto the South Eastern Division. Presumably the veteran 6-CORs, which were as old as many of the SED's former steam-hauled carriages, were the only stock available to form additional peak-hour and boat train services. During the spring of 1967 the units could be seen on driving training trips, one of their first recorded revenue-earning workings being on 17th June when Nos. 3046/49 formed the 2.05pm (SO) Ramsgate to Victoria. From the start of a new timetable on 10th July 1967 four 12-car sets were reported to be in use on commuter trains on the division. The units were still active on the SED during 1968, but by then were largely confined to seasonal extra workings, such as a Herne Bay to Victoria and return special on 11th July conveying French students. On 18th August 1968 a pair of 6-CORs worked the 11.10am from Victoria to Ramsgate. The SED's rolling stock resources must have really been stretched to the limit during that month, because on various dates two 6-CORs were booked to form the 7.30am Victoria to Folkestone Harbour boat train. They reportedly required the assistance of a locomotive to return up the 1 in 30 gradient of the harbour branch, from where they were officially prohibited. In this shot unit No.3049 is seen bouncing along at the approach to Shortlands with a Victoria to Ramsgate train some time during the summer of 1968. One dreads to think what the passengers thought of the 'new' Kent Coast rolling stock. All of the units were withdrawn in April 1969 and subsequently broken-up at such far-flung locations as Stockton-on-Tees. *Ken Wightman*

A Charing Cross to Ramsgate (via Chatham) train is seen at St Mary Cray Junction some time during the spring of 1974. The leading unit is 2-HAP No.6051, out-shopped in January 1959 and one of a sizeable batch (Nos. 6043 to 6105) ordered for use on Phase One of the Kent Coast electrification. It is recorded that it spent a period in store at Gatwick sidings prior to entering traffic. These units comprised of a motor second brake with two separate second class saloons, each seating 42 passengers, and a driving trailer composite. The latter coach had 50 second class seats in a saloon with 19 first class seats in compartments. Between the two sections were two lavatories, one for each class, the first class toilet being reached by a short corridor. *Ken Smith*

Another shot of a 2-HAP unit, this time showing No.6012 on the Chislehurst loop line with a Margate to Charing Cross (via Maidstone East) train in September 1971. The leading coach is a driving trailer composite vehicle (described in the previous caption) and the position of the first class accommodation and toilet can be clearly seen. It should be noted that unit Nos. 6001 to 6105 had Mk.4 motor and trailer bogies while the later 2-HAP stock (unit Nos. 6106 to 6173) had the more modern Commonwealth trailer bogies, which were in favour on BR at the time, and Mk.3B motor bogies. Towards the end of its career No.6012 was paired with No.6036 and formed into 4-CAP four-car unit No.3207. It finished its working life on the South Eastern Division. *Ken Smith*

A Maidstone East to Victoria train, led by 2-HAL unit No.2675, heads for London at St Mary Cray Junction on 14th June 1958. The unsightly earthworks in the background are a result of the considerable amount of civil engineering work that was taking place in this area before the inauguration of Phase One of the Kent Coast electrification scheme. The five-miles long section of line between Bickley Junction and Swanley Junction was quadrupled, and many associated spur lines in the Bickley Junction area were remodelled to ease speed restrictions. The year 1959 was destined to be the last that 2-HALs operated on the SED, because they were progressively replaced by 2-HAPs as these became available. A few 2-HALs reportedly lingered on some Victoria to Ramsgate services until the autumn of 1959. *R. C. Riley*

For more than forty years 4-EPB units formed the backbone of suburban services on the South Eastern Division, while the Kent Coast services were largely dominated by 4-CEP stock for a similar period. Here, in a typical scene from that time, 4-EPB No.5191, forming a Blackfriars to Sevenoaks service, and 4-CEP No.7176, on a Victoria to Ramsgate train, run neck and neck near Swanley in the summer of 1975. *Ken Smith*

'Sittingbourne, you change here for Queenborough and Sheerness', was the usual greeting awaiting passengers at the north Kent town, whether or not a connecting train was advertised! 4-CEP No.7177 runs in leading the 10.40am Victoria to Ramsgate train, which will detach a portion for Dover Marine at Faversham. There was always a booked connection with the fast off-peak services, and for passengers heading for the Isle of Sheppey there is a train formed of two 2-HAP units waiting in the adjacent platform. This portrait was taken on 7th April 1973. No.7177 was one of a sizeable batch of units (Nos. 7154 to 7204) built in 1960/61 for Phase Two of the Kent Coast electrification scheme. Like the earlier Phase One stock, they consisted of a motor second brake, trailer composite corridor, trailer second corridor and another motor second brake. This gave a total of 24 first class and 200 second class seats, although it should be mentioned that later there were one or two units with a slightly different layout. For example, in unit No.7189 the trailer second was a former composite coach, this reform being the result of fire damage. The most noticeable difference between the Phase One and Two units was the bogies, the former having Mk.4 motor and trailer bogies, while the latter had Mk.3B motor and Commonwealth trailer bogies. The Phase Two stock also had a number of internal improvements, such as the design of the first class seating. *Chris Evans*

In the 1970s a number of additional workings to the Kent seaside resorts were run at weekends and Bank Holidays, some of them being normal service trains extended to the coast with their booked suburban stock. In this case the regular 9.30am Charing Cross to Dartford has had its journey increased from just 17 miles to almost 80, and the hardy pleasure-seekers have had to endure two-and-a-quarter hours in non-corridor stock without toilet facilities (no doubt it would have seemed twice as long on the journey home). Hardly the perfect way to start or finish a day out by the sea! This picture was taken at precisely 11.46am on 25th August 1975 and shows unit Nos. 5186 and 5206 running into Westgate-on-Sea, the last stop before Margate, which was no doubt the destination for most of the trippers. The train would then have continued to Ramsgate where it would have berthed for the evening return working. *Chris Evans*

The final batch of 41 4-VEP units was initially allocated to Ramsgate and unit No.7868 was only a few months old when photographed starting out from its home station with the 11.23am to Charing Cross on 2nd March 1974. This picture gives an excellent view of the track layout and installations at the west end of the station, showing the emu inspection shed (to quote its official title), and station in the right background. It is not immediately apparent from this picture, but all of the railway facilities seen here are of relatively recent origin. Remarkably, the two pre-grouping companies that served this area had separate stations in Ramsgate, so one of the first acts of the newly-formed Southern Railway was to construct a new station to unify the two systems. The existing station premises, and adjacent steam engine sheds plus carriage sidings, were opened on the site seen here in 1926, the only disadvantage of which was the station's remoteness from the town centre and seashore. *Chris Evans*

When this picture was taken at Ramsgate emu inspection shed on 27th May 1959 steam traction was very much on its 'last legs' in the area and, in fact, only had about 2½ weeks to run in regular service. Part of the new maintenance facilities for electric stock are seen here, note the spotless pits, which enable staff to examine a unit's running gear, and the premises' light and airy appearance which was no doubt in contrast to the grimy steam shed! This picture was actually taken in the new 'lifting' shop where coaches could be separated from their bogies to enable motors and wheels to be changed. Some of the old steam shed buildings (which were quite recently built, as previously mentioned) were incorporated in the modern new depot and remain in use today. The 'train' in the shot consists of a 350hp diesel shunter hauling a 'dead' 2-HAP unit in connection with (electrical pick-up) shoe clearance tests, presumably prior to the depot being fully commissioned. *John Langford*

Faversham to Dover

Canterbury East is the distinctive location for this shot of 4-CEP No.7182 leaving the station with a Victoria to Dover working on a sunny October afternoon in 1969. Note the signal box which is located atop a gantry. Judging by the pile of sleepers, in the background, the goods yard tracks appear to have been recently lifted. The author recalls that No.7182 was one of a number of 4-CEP units that were considerably overdue for heavy body overhaul at the time of this picture, hence it was still in green livery. It was delivered in January 1961 and in normal circumstances would have received a heavy repair after 7½ years, but this was delayed, apparently by a shortage of workshop capacity caused by the reorganisation of Eastleigh Works. The internal condition of those units outstanding for works' attention left much to be desired, especially the dreadful state of their upholstery after over eight years of intensive use. *Author*

Sittingbourne to Sheerness

During the time when the Kent Coast electrification scheme was progressing, criticism was sometimes heard that some lightly-trafficked lines were being electrified when, if they had been located elsewhere in Great Britain, they would probably have been candidates for closure. The accusation was, of course, that routes in the south-east of England close to the capital were being given preferential treatment. It is certainly difficult to see how electrification of the Ashford to Ramsgate via Canterbury West or the Paddock Wood to Strood lines was justified in financial terms, neither of them passing through large towns not already served by other routes. Another 'lucky' line was the Sittingbourne to Sheerness-on-Sea branch which was electrified in 1959 as part of the Phase One Kent Coast scheme. It must be admitted, however, that this line now boasts a frequent half-hourly service and is probably more prosperous than at any time in the past. In this picture its Sheerness terminal station is seen in 1968 with 2-HAP unit No.6138, one of the later units with Commonwealth trailer bogies, nearest to the camera. *Colour-Rail*

Electrification of suburban lines in the 1920s/30s led to a massive growth in the number of people commuting into London, for example weekday arrivals at Charing Cross and Cannon Street were 16,000 in 1925 and 34,000 in 1935. Many of the South Eastern suburban lines had been resignalled with colour lights in the 1920s, so there was little scope for increasing line capacity, and longer trains would have entailed huge expenditure on new track layouts and station reconstruction and this option was also ruled out. The 'Southern' still wished to provide a seat for everyone if at all possible, and in 1941 the first of the new 4-SUB units appeared, offering 468 seats per unit. This very high seating capacity was, however, achieved (as mentioned elsewhere in this book) by cramming passengers into very narrow, uncomfortable compartments and these units were decidedly unpopular as a result. In his quest to provide more seats, Oliver Bulleid designed a revolutionary, at least by British standards, double-deck train consisting of two 4-coach units. The units were in the traditional form with a motor coach at each end and two trailer vehicles formed intermediately. Strictly speaking it was not a true double-decker like those to be found on European railways where the loading gauge is much more generous, but a '1½ decker', because the upper compartments were only a few feet above the lower ones. Access to the upper accommodation was by a short staircase from an adjoining lower compartment. Each unit provided 552 seats, which was not a great increase on the first ten 4-SUB units. Due to tight clearances the upper windows could not be opened and the compartments were pressure-ventilated, but this equipment proved to be troublesome from the outset and was the units' 'Achilles heel' throughout their lives. Another problem concerned the long loading times at station stops and this had the effect of slightly reducing line capacity, thus defeating the whole object of trying to provide extra seats, so it was decided that no further double-deck trains would be introduced. For most of their careers the units were confined to rush-hour only workings, based on Slade Green depot, but their use during the height of the peaks was avoided due to the loading difficulties previously mentioned. The units were withdrawn in October 1971, and three vehicles were subsequently privately preserved. In this picture units 4002/01 are seen awaiting departure from Charing Cross with the 8.27am to Slade Green on 22nd June 1970. *Colour-Rail*

South Eastern Suburban

In late 1970 the double-deck units were renumbered 4901/4902 and repainted in blue livery with full yellow ends. This shot, taken at Eltham Well Hall in May 1971, gives a close up view of the layout of this stock with alternating lower and upper compartments. The latter must have been particularly claustrophobic!
John Edgington

A Charing Cross to Hayes train, formed of BR Standard 4-EPB unit No.5344, rounds the curve at the approach to London Bridge on 1st October 1972. This unit was one of 54 sets built at Eastleigh Carriage Works for the South Eastern Division in 1960–62 and, in addition, a further 14 sets were constructed for the South Western Division in 1963. The unit numbers were 5303 to 5356 and 5357 to 5370 respectively. It should be noted that the first two units in this number series, Nos. 5301 and 5302, were replacements for Southern Railway-designed units that had been partly written off following accident damage. They had BR Standard motor coaches and 'Southern' trailers. The 'production series' of BR sets was unlike their forerunners in many major respects. The older Southern Railway-designed 4-EPBs had the familiar curved body shape and used a 'Southern' underframe and bogies. The BR-designed stock naturally employed a BR Standard underframe, different body profile plus bogies, and even had a revised internal layout and design. The original units' passenger accommodation consisted of two completely open motor coaches plus a trailer coach with a similar layout, the other trailer being of the compartment type. The BR units had semi-saloon motor coaches, while the trailer vehicles broke new ground for the SR in that both had a mix of compartment and saloon seating. The total seating capacity of these units was 392. *Gerald Daniels*

It would be a considerable understatement to say that this general view of the 'South Eastern' side of London Bridge station has changed since this scene was recorded in the late 1950s. Needless to say, the skyline is, sadly, no longer dominated by the dome of St Paul's Cathedral and the dockside cranes have long since disappeared. The station has, of course, been totally rebuilt. Improvements included the easing of the tight curves seen here, a new up through road and wider footbridges and stairways, all of these making the premises much more convenient to use. All the rolling stock has been consigned to history, the 4-EPBs' final revenue-earning trips taking place on 31st March 1995. *R. C. Riley*

An unidentified 4-EPB unit, which has the early style 'S' prefix to its unit number, is pictured between Hither Green and Grove Park stations in the late 1950s. The headcode denotes a Cannon Street to Bromley North service. The wisps of steam above the third carriage indicate the site of Hither Green motive power depot, while a main line steam train can just be discerned in the background. The tracks to the marshalling yard can be seen behind the signal on the right of the shot. Despite being commonplace on the SR for more than a generation, these units rarely attracted the attention of railway enthusiasts, and it is likely that in this case the photographer was present to record the passing of the steam train, rather than the humble 4-EPB unit. *R. C. Riley*

A Victoria to Orpington train, formed of 4-EPB unit No.5174, rattles along between Shortlands and Bromley South stations in April 1975. These reliable and unsophisticated units were part of the everyday scene for more than forty years. The tall chimney, partially visible in the background, is a well-known landmark for railway travellers, and forms part of Valley Road pumping station. *Ken Smith*

A view of the 'country end' of Bromley South station on 6th June 1959 showing 4-SUB unit No.4101 leaving with a Holborn Viaduct to Sevenoaks service via the Catford loop. The steam train, which was doubtless of much greater interest to the photographer, is the 10.35am Victoria to Ramsgate headed by Maunsell 'Schools' Class 4-4-0 No.30915 *Brighton*. No.4101 entered service on the Victoria to Orpington route, which was an especially busy one, where the suburban numerical headcodes were used for the first time. The unit's wide, rounded body profile, which was quite different from previous traditional designs, must have made quite an impression on travellers. No.4101 was completed with first class accommodation, but in October 1941 all London suburban services became 'third class only' and its first class seating was downgraded prior to the unit entering traffic. No.4101 was withdrawn in May 1972 after more than 30 years' service. *Colour-Rail*

The Kent Coast electrification entailed considerable remodelling of track layouts in order to speed-up services and provide additional capacity through bottlenecks. Some of the most extensive work was carried out between Bickley Junction and Swanley Junction, where the lines to Chatham and Maidstone diverge, this section of line being quadrupled. This work involved the reconstruction of St Mary Cray station which was enlarged to accommodate two extra tracks. In this shot the new buildings look attractive enough and it appears that, judging by the rusty surface of the rails, the platform on which the photographer stood to take this picture was not yet operational. Note that vegetation had not yet grown up on the side of the newly excavated cutting, on the right, which looks remarkably neat and tidy. Despite the huge investment in new infrastructure and main-line rolling stock, South Eastern Division suburban services were left largely untouched and the unit seen here on 8th May 1959 is 4-SUB No.4387, some of which were still active on the Division at that time. The headcode indicates a Sevenoaks to Holborn Viaduct train via the Catford loop. Regular 4-SUB workings on the 'South Eastern' are understood to have been phased out later during 1959, although there was reportedly a booked diagram for a 4-SUB on a mail train to Dartford until 1971 and, of course, they frequently visited Slade Green repair shop for overhaul. *R. C. Riley*

A scene recorded at St Mary Cray Junction on 23rd May 1959 showing 4-SUB unit No.4343 heading towards London with the 3.42pm Sevenoaks to Holborn Viaduct train. This unit was originally one of the '1496' Class three-car units built in 1925 for the Eastern Section, but in the mid-1940s was augmented by the addition of a steel-bodied trailer and renumbered. Note the 'H' headcode, but do not overlook the dot above it, which was an important part of the indication. This code indicated a Sevenoaks to Holborn Viaduct train routed via Swanley and Nunhead. This was one of the routes where the letter headcodes displayed by up and down trains bore no resemblance to each other, and a train travelling in the reverse direction would have carried the letter 'S' with a bar above it. One wonders how today's commuters would react to such a convoluted (or maybe 'dotty'!) system. *Neil Sprinks*

A 4-SUB deep in 'South Eastern' territory! In this vintage view 4-SUB unit No.4706 is depicted south of Eynsford with a Holborn Viaduct to Sevenoaks working on a lovely autumn day in 1957. These units were, almost needless to say, not compatible with 4-EPB/2-EPB stock, which comprised by far the greater part of the SED's fleet at that time, and this must have caused the operating authorities a considerable headache when the train service was disrupted. One wonders how many times a 4-SUB got onto the wrong diagram and was booked to form an eight-car train with a 4-EPB during its travels! *Neil Sprinks*

A Blackfriars to Sevenoaks train via the Catford loop, led by former 'Tyneside' 2-EPB unit No.5783 in green livery, is depicted rounding the curve after leaving Nunhead on 21st April 1968. The rear unit is a standard SR set in blue livery. The line in the background is the erstwhile branch from Nunhead to Greenwich Park which was closed in 1917, but was subsequently partially reopened. In 1929 a connection was laid from the dormant branch to Lewisham station to give transfer freight trains easier access to Hither Green yard. This new connection was later electrified primarily for use by rush-hour passenger services from Holborn Viaduct to the Dartford lines. *Chris Gammell*

Maintenance and Repair

The SR's rolling stock maintenance policy in the early 1960s was once described as one of 'systematic decay', doubtless a result of the responsibilities being shared among various offices at different locations. Certainly there was little co-ordination until the establishment of a new rolling stock maintenance control section (Maintrol) at Croydon in 1971, which brought the fleet under much stricter control. Here Chris Evans, who was closely involved with establishing the new organisation, outlines the deficiencies of the old system and benefits plus the maintenance policies of the new organisation.

Of all forms of traction in this country the SR's electric multiple units are perhaps the least changed of any in almost one hundred years of evolution. 2003 was the centennial year of Parliamentary approval being granted to the LBSCR for electrification of the whole of their system, and the company first began running electric trains in 1909. Those pioneering multiple units worked on the overhead contact system (arguably more efficient than the third rail in use today), and the 6,600-volt supply was transformed to 750 volts for traction, exactly the same as currently (pun intended!) used. There was a transformer supplying the auxiliary equipment, which included Westinghouse air compressors little different from those still in use today. Of all the systems perhaps only the control equipment can be said to have evolved to any substantial degree. Even the coach dimensions were within inches of being the same as stock running almost one hundred years later!

Part of the lifting shop at Eastleigh works, where coaches are lifted off their bogies (by the overhead travelling crane in the background). By the time they arrive here, units have been completely split up (as can be seen), their coaches not even necessarily in the same shop at the same time. On the right are Mk.6 motor bogies, re-assembled after cleaning and with overhauled brake rigging, newly-turned or re-tyred wheel-sets and traction motors which will have been dismantled, field tested and had the armature commutators skimmed. The picture was taken on 17th September 1974. *Chris Evans*

That the SR emus still active today are basically very little changed from those early units is due in part to the natural longevity of this type of traction. It is often said that few steam locomotives of any age retained many original moving parts by the time they were withdrawn, and here is a parallel in that during the course of its life a typical twentieth-century emu will have kept few, if any, of its original electrical fittings. Also, just as some steam engines – notably the Bulleid Pacifics – were rebuilt as effectively new locomotives, so some multiple units have had their lives extended by refurbishment, both of passenger accommodation and electrical equipment.

The everyday maintenance of steam locomotives has been chronicled many times, but very little has ever been written about what went on behind the scenes in keeping the SR's emu fleet running: this was the responsibility of the region's Chief Mechanical & Electrical Engineer's (CM&EE) Department. Until 1966 the CM&EE's headquarters had been at London Bridge, whilst drawing offices were still at workshops sites which included Ashford, Brighton, Lancing and Eastleigh; at the last-mentioned was also the headquarters of the Carriage & Wagon (C&W) department. From this it will not perhaps be surprising that the relationship between these far-removed departments was neither good, bad nor indifferent, but virtually non-existent! There was a great coming-together in 1966, when the C&W was absorbed by the CM&EE at a new headquarters in Croydon.

For the first five years there was an uneasy co-existence between the erstwhile separate departments, although the former London Bridge sections (responsible for the day-to-day maintenance requirements of the emu fleet) and the ex-Eastleigh contingent (directing longer-term inspection and shopping procedures) were located on different, albeit neighbouring, floors. Furthermore, the Control staff, who had the job of putting the plans into action, were located ten storeys away! Under the old system, whenever a vehicle was taken out of service for a defect that might call for a repair beyond the capability of the local depot, or when a passenger stock unit, coach or van neared its shopping proposal 'SP' date, a rolling stock inspector would be despatched to fill in a 'Shopping Proposal' form. This was a comprehensive document which required a thorough examination of the vehicle concerned, covering virtually every aspect of its mechanical and physical condition.

The shopping proposal forms would arrive at the shopping bureau in great bundles for examination by technical managers, who would compare the repair requirements and condition with the 'SP' date and sagely determine whether the unit or vehicle concerned should have a scheduled overhaul, be sent to a repair shop for an unclassified repair, or perhaps remain in traffic. This could often be something of a lottery, depending on the perceived condition of the stock concerned and the availability of suitable capacity at the proposed works or repair shop. The haphazard method of shopping, with little forward planning – and absolutely no co-ordination with the routine depot repairs – meant that some units ran well past their 'SP' dates and, perhaps because they were mechanically in good condition, were sometimes left to run in traffic whilst in a pretty awful state inside.

All this made for everyday problems with the practicalities of maintaining the fleet, and it rapidly became apparent that something would have to be done to properly co-ordinate activities. The result was the establishment of a new Maintenance Control (Maintrol) section in 1971, and I, along with the author, witnessed its sometimes painful gestation from what had earlier been an incredibly diverse and widely-spread range of activities.

Maintrol brought together all of the aforementioned functions in a single section (and all on one floor) and within a very short time it became apparent that the new organisation was what had been needed all along. At the time there was still an amazingly diverse collection of emu stock in operation on the SR, ranging from pre-war wooden-bodied 4-COR stock (albeit in its last year of service) to 4-CIGs and 4-VEPs which, although designed almost a decade earlier, were still being built in some quantity. One of the most fascinating aspects of working in Maintrol at the time was that all of this stock had its own particular maintenance requirements, for although in many respects all the types were electrically quite similar there were disparities in design features, usage and mileage which necessitated differing repairs, both planned and unscheduled.

Planned repairs were divided into two categories, long-term maintenance (LTM) and short-term maintenance (STM). A typical sequence of LTM repairs to a main-line unit would be C1-C4-C3-C4-C3-C4-C1, at roughly 15-monthly intervals. To take the lesser repairs first, the C4 (or 'GO' – General Overhaul) was normally carried out at Chart Leacon (Ashford) repair shop, and involved lifting the coach bodies off the bogies, which were then reconditioned with their wheel-sets, along with the motors, motor generators, compressors and batteries. The brake gear was also stripped and overhauled, then thoroughly tested before the unit was returned to service. C1 (heavy) and C3 (intermediate) repairs were almost exclusively carried out at main workshops, usually Eastleigh, and included all the work involved in a C4 plus, in the case of a C3, necessary body repairs (both externally and internally) and normally a full repaint. The C1 repair included a complete body overhaul, repaint and re-upholstery of the seats. Most suburban units ran a considerably lower mileage than main-line stock, with a greater proportion of the fleet running only in the peak-hours, and here the 'GO' was usually carried out at Slade Green repair shop, near Dartford, at around two-yearly intervals. Instead of a C3 repair most of these units received a C6, which was roughly the equivalent of a C3 but without any of the overhaul element of a C4, and the coaches were not lifted. These repairs were carried out in a substantial paint shop occupying part of the Selhurst complex, near Croydon. There was also a repair shop here, but it rarely received units for C4 repairs but instead was kept busy with a considerable number of the unscheduled C5s, which arose when a component defect required a coach to be lifted. This may have been simply to change a failed motor, or perhaps a couple of wheel-sets with 'flats' caused by sliding on the rails, but sometimes could be a much bigger repair following a mishap. Chart Leacon and Slade Green also dealt with these un-programmed repairs, which were generally known as 'side jobs' (the 'C' repair notation being confined to main works repairs).

Unlike at Eastleigh works, where units were split and their coaches often to be found in different shops, at Chart Leacon repair shop it was the usual practice for a four-car set to occupy a single road. The overhead lifting cranes can be seen in this picture of 4-BIG No.7051 undergoing a General Overhaul: in front of the unit is a pair of Mk.6 motor wheel-sets. The repair shop was divided into the 'north-side' and 'south-side', the former dealing with the later B5-bogie stock and the latter with all other main-line types, together with DEMUs and some of the BR Standard 4-EPBs. In a typical week Chart Leacon was capable of overhauling no less than twelve 4-car units, each complete lift being accomplished within an eight-hour shift, and this quick turn-around could only, of course, be achieved by exchanging all the removed components (bogies, wheel-sets, motors, generators, compressors and batteries) for a reconditioned set, which would have been removed from a similar unit some days earlier. Before being returned to traffic, the unit would move to the adjacent inspection shed to receive a 'Shed' and CPM and have all the brake, electrical and air systems tested. *Chris Evans*

STM (short-term maintenance) was completed at the various inspection sheds dotted around the region, which are the modern equivalent of the old steam motive power depots. Here the principal repair was known somewhat esoterically as a 'Shed', and would be carried out at roughly three- or four-monthly intervals. It involved the examination of the control and brake gear, air systems and associated electrical equipment, and usually a change of motor brushes. Then at monthly intervals there was a CPM (carriage preventive maintenance) repair, which included the examination of – and any necessary repair to – bodywork, upholstery and interior fittings, as well as the heating and lighting systems. An important aspect of this job was checking the action of door locks and making any necessary adjustments. At the same interval, although not usually at the same time, those units fitted with white-metal axle bearings would have their axle-boxes topped up with oil. Again, much of the inspection shed's time would be taken up with non-planned work, such as with broken or defective fittings, and mechanical or electrical components, although there was no specific name given to such casual jobs.

With the inauguration of Maintrol, defects were reported day or night to the Control staff, who would initially liaise with their traffic colleagues when the failure occurred whilst the unit concerned was in service, and in some cases arrange for repairs to be carried out without delay. Otherwise, the unit would be included in a list of 'stopped' units compiled at the beginning of service each morning. This list was duplicated for easy visual reference in the form of a large wall-mounted display, which instantly gave a snapshot of every unit out of traffic, by location and defect or scheduled repair type. Each unit class was colour-coded, so that it was possible to see at a glance which had been most severely affected by overnight 'stoppages': the sight of four 4-REPs out of service, for instance (eight of the original eleven units were diagrammed), would immediately provoke looks of consternation all round! Also, the number of units under repair at any particular depot could be assessed and taken into consideration when planning where to send units requiring attention.

Remarkably, in pre-Maintrol days the SR had managed its fleet without finding the need to allocate the majority of emu stock to any specific depot: only certain specialised types had been specifically identified with a particular 'home'. A measure of the tighter control that Maintrol facilitated, however, was that it was soon possible to allocate every unit; as well as making it much easier to identify shortages or surpluses for any given group of services. This also had the great spin-off advantage of making each depot responsible for its own stock: there could be no more 'Oh, just fix it with a piece of string tonight, Charlie, it'll be somebody else's problem tomorrow!'

The allocation of stock to depots enabled far more rigorous control of the fleet – which had been Maintrol's principal objective – and it was then possible to set availability targets and to monitor performance so that shortfalls or surpluses could be quickly identified. These benefits were a small price to pay for a slight loss in flexibility, and in due course availability averages of around 88% became the standard, at least for the larger fleets. This may seem quite low compared with some of today's figures, but it should be remembered that this was at a time when repaints – requiring about two weeks out of service – were routinely carried out at 2½-yearly intervals and GOs every 100,000 miles (the comparable periods today are about ten years and nearer to 200,000 miles, if at all). Collision damage could have a considerable, and often long-term, effect on availability, but often it was possible to re-form the units involved so that a serviceable one could be made up from the undamaged coaches of one or two others. This could result in hybrid units appearing with coaches from a different class, although the scope for this was limited by such factors as electrical or brake compatibility.

Another ploy was to re-allocate units between depots to make up for temporary shortfalls, and this was most often used when a series of newer stock (such as the 4-CIGs and 4-VEPs), which had been allocated to several depots in numerical blocks, became due for main works repair at about the same time. The resultant transfers, and subsequent re-transfers, must

A confusing picture, inside Slade Green repair shop, which at first sight appears to show 4-VEP No.7852 undergoing extensive surgery: in fact it is driving trailer coach S76620 of 4-CIG No.7346 which was being fitted with one of unit No.7852's cab ends following collision damage. No.7346 was badly damaged in a collision at Wimbledon Park in 1975 whilst No.7852 was partly gutted by fire at Effingham Junction on 24th November 1973. The latter was almost brand new at the time. The photograph clearly shows the sort of extensive body repair capabilities at this location. *Chris Evans*

sometimes have been accompanied by much puzzlement among the 'spotters' of the day, but these moves returned much of the flexibility of the time before depot allocation.

I hope the above gives the reader some sort of insight into the often colourful daily process that befell the CM&EE in maintaining sufficient stock for service, sometimes against all the odds. The task can perhaps be best summarised by imagining you are seated at a desk in front of a board awash with the many colours of 'stopped' unit cards on some wet and windy autumn morning, as in one ear you hear a barrage of protest from a harassed traffic controller who has just had to run two consecutive morning peak trains short of stock on the Brighton Line, whilst in the other an equally irate depot manager is protesting that half of his morning shift are sitting around playing cards because the units promised for them to work on have not arrived! Throughout this album you will find obvious instances of irregular workings or formations which will have been brought about by some minor crisis, perhaps many months earlier. There may also have been a background story behind many of the seemingly ordered shots of trains going about their business, but I can now, perhaps, leave that to your imagination …

The SR's emus – or indeed small fleets of electric and electro-diesel locomotives – have never enjoyed the same attraction and following as have steam classes. But for decades now they have been quietly serving one of the most densely populated areas in the world and there can be few people in the south east of England who have never travelled on one, and even fewer who have never seen one! That they are not all the same and have a unique appeal of their own is, I think, apparent in this fine selection of photographs.

In the paint shop at Selhurst, which dealt principally with suburban units, 4-SUB Nos. 4277 and 4290 are receiving a C6 repaint. The cab ends are being treated following airless spraying of the bodysides. Until the mid-1960s and the advent of corporate blue, most stock receiving intermediate repairs here would not have been externally repainted but have had the (green) paintwork cleaned and re-varnished, to a very high-quality finish. *Chris Evans*

Front cover An Aldershot to Guildford train, with 2-HAL unit No.2639 leading, leaves Wanborough on 15th June 1963. This unit, like most of this stock, was built in 1938 for the Gillingham/Maidstone electrification, and this particular example lasted in traffic until 1969. *Trevor Owen*

Title page Photographed in the days when green livery was still in favour on the Southern Region, this detailed general view of the approach to Waterloo Station, taken in 1965, is really worth a second glance. The train in the foreground is an up Windsor Line suburban working formed of 4-SUB stock, whilst (what appears to be) a down Portsmouth train, composed of 4-COR units, is leaving the station, with another suburban working behind it. Sandwiched between them are the rear coaches of an up steam-hauled train, which, rather unusually, has a maroon-liveried first class coach in its formation. This fascinating shot was taken from an ideally positioned block of flats, but the activities of the railway photographers did not always meet with the approval of the residents and ugly confrontations sometimes occurred. Perhaps a small charge for admission would have placated them! *John Hayward*

Back cover A fast Victoria to Brighton train is seen at the approach to Clayton Tunnel, with 4-CIG unit No.7318 leading; the rear unit also appears to be a 4-CIG. This illustration, which was taken on 12th March 1967, shows how smart the 4-CIG/4-BIG units looked in the SR green livery. In the author's view a couple of yellow bodyside stripes would have further improved the appearance of this stock. Despite the fact that the train is not far from the outer suburbs of Brighton, the line is climbing on a gradient of 1 in 264 against southbound trains, although it is unlikely that passengers would have noticed any reduction in speed! The gradient changes to 1 in 264 downhill at the southern end of Clayton tunnel about 1½ miles from where this scene was recorded. *Gerald Daniels*